# Cooking For Two

## Recipes

**Delectable Dishes for You and Me**

**Copyright-All Rights Reserved**

This book has copyright protection. You can use the book for personal purpose. You should not see, use, alter, distribute, quote, take excerpts or paraphrase in part or whole the material contained in this book without obtaining the permission of the author first.

# Contents

Introduction .................... 1

Chapter 1: Breakfast .................. 3

Chapter 2: Soups And Sandwiches ... 13

Chapter 3: Salads .................. 24

Chapter 4: Seafood .................. 30

Chapter 5: Meat .................. 37

Chapter 6: Snacks & Sides .......... 45

Chapter 7: Dessert .................. 54

Thank you .................. 70

# Introduction

Welcome to "Cooking for Two Recipes" - a culinary journey that celebrates the joy of preparing delicious meals while being mindful of portion sizes and minimizing food waste. In a world where both time and resources are valuable commodities, this cookbook is your ultimate guide to creating mouthwatering dishes tailored perfectly for two.

Cooking for two comes with a unique set of challenges and opportunities. It's a chance to embrace creativity, savor intimacy, and make the most of each ingredient. In this cookbook, we've curated a collection of recipes that are not only designed to cater to your tastes but also respect your resources.

Each recipe has been thoughtfully crafted to offer a harmonious blend of flavors, textures, and nutrients while ensuring that you're left with minimal leftovers. We understand the frustration of throwing away excess ingredients, and that's why these recipes are a delightful solution. With our easy-to-follow instructions and perfectly portioned ingredients, you'll discover a new world of cooking that's not only convenient but also eco-conscious.

Gone are the days of trying to downsize recipes meant for a crowd. Here, you'll find a variety of dishes – from cozy dinners to romantic desserts – all tailored for two hungry souls. Embrace the joy of cooking without the pressure of excessive leftovers, and relish in the satisfaction of preparing meals that are just right for you and your partner.

Join us in the kitchen as we embark on this culinary adventure that champions intimacy, simplicity, and the art of cooking without waste. Let "Cooking for Two Recipes" be your trusted companion as you explore the pleasures of cooking and sharing meals that truly matter.

# Scrambled Eggs with Vegetables

Ingredients:

4 large eggs
1/4 cup bell peppers (any color), diced
1/4 cup onion, diced
1/4 cup tomatoes, diced
1/4 cup spinach, chopped
1/4 cup shredded cheese (cheddar, mozzarella, or your choice)
2 tablespoons butter or cooking oil
Salt and pepper to taste
Chopped fresh herbs (such as parsley or chives) for garnish (optional)

Instructions:
Prep the Vegetables:
Dice the bell peppers, onions, and tomatoes into small pieces.
Chop the spinach.
If using herbs for garnish, chop them as well.
Whisk the Eggs:
Crack the eggs into a bowl.
Season with a pinch of salt and a dash of black pepper.
Whisk the eggs until the yolks and whites are well combined.
Sauté the Vegetables:
In a non-stick skillet, heat the butter or cooking oil over medium heat.
Add the diced onions and bell peppers. Sauté for about 2-3 minutes until they start to soften.
Add Tomatoes and Spinach:
Add the diced tomatoes to the skillet. Cook for an additional 1-2 minutes until they release some of their juices.
Add the chopped spinach and cook for another 1-2 minutes until wilted.
Pour the Eggs:
Push the sautéed vegetables to one side of the skillet.
Pour the whisked eggs into the empty side of the skillet.
Scramble the Eggs:
Let the eggs sit for a few seconds until they start to set around the edges.
Gently scramble the eggs with a spatula, mixing them with the sautéed vegetables. Continue cooking and stirring occasionally until the eggs are cooked to your desired level of doneness.
Add Cheese:
Sprinkle the shredded cheese over the scrambled eggs.
Stir gently until the cheese is melted and incorporated into the eggs.
Serve:
Divide the scrambled eggs with vegetables between two plates.
Serve hot with toast, tortillas, or any preferred side dish.
Enjoy your delicious and nutritious Scrambled Eggs with Vegetables for a satisfying breakfast or brunch for two!

# Quinoa-Pear Breakfast Bake

Ingredients:

For the Quinoa-Pear Bake:
1/2 cup quinoa, rinsed and drained
1 cup milk (dairy or non-dairy)
1 ripe pear, peeled, cored, and diced
2 tablespoons pure maple syrup or honey
1/2 teaspoon vanilla extract
1/2 teaspoon ground cinnamon
1/4 teaspoon ground nutmeg
Pinch of salt

For the Topping:

1/4 cup chopped nuts (e.g., walnuts, almonds, or pecans)
2 tablespoons old-fashioned oats
1 tablespoon brown sugar
1/2 tablespoon butter, melted
Pinch of ground cinnamon

Instructions:

Preheat the Oven:
Preheat your oven to 350°F (175°C).
Prepare Quinoa:
In a medium saucepan, combine the rinsed quinoa and milk. Bring to a gentle boil over medium heat. Reduce the heat to low, cover the saucepan, and let the quinoa simmer for about 15 minutes, or until most of the liquid is absorbed and the quinoa is cooked.
Mix in Pear and Flavors:
Stir in the diced pear, maple syrup or honey, vanilla extract, ground cinnamon, ground nutmeg, and a pinch of salt into the cooked quinoa.
Prepare Topping:

In a small bowl, mix together the chopped nuts, oats, brown sugar, melted butter, and a pinch of ground cinnamon.
Assemble and Bake:
Divide the quinoa-pear mixture between two oven-safe ramekins or a small baking dish for two. Sprinkle the nut and oat topping evenly over the quinoa-pear mixture.
Bake:
Place the ramekins or baking dish in the preheated oven.
Bake for about 20-25 minutes, or until the top is golden brown and the mixture is heated through.
Serve:

# Salmon Croquette Sandwiches

Ingredients:

For the Salmon Croquettes:
1 can (14.75 oz) pink or red salmon, drained and flaked
1/4 cup breadcrumbs
1 egg, beaten
2 tablespoons mayonnaise
2 tablespoons finely chopped onion
1 tablespoon chopped fresh parsley
1/2 teaspoon Dijon mustard
1/2 teaspoon lemon juice
Salt and pepper to taste
2 tablespoons cooking oil (for frying)

For the Sandwiches:

4 slices of your favorite bread (whole wheat, sourdough, etc.)
Lettuce leaves
Sliced tomatoes
Sliced red onion
Additional mayonnaise or tartar sauce (optional)

Instructions:

Prepare the Salmon Croquette Mixture:
In a mixing bowl, combine the flaked salmon, breadcrumbs, beaten egg, mayonnaise, chopped onion, chopped parsley, Dijon mustard, lemon juice, salt, and pepper.
Mix the ingredients until well combined. If the mixture is too wet, you can add a bit more breadcrumbs to help bind it.
Shape and Fry the Croquettes:
Divide the salmon mixture into two portions and shape them into patties.
In a skillet, heat the cooking oil over medium heat.
Carefully place the salmon patties in the skillet and cook for about 3-4 minutes on each side, or until they are golden brown and heated through. Make sure they are cooked evenly on both sides.
Assemble the Sandwiches:
Toast the slices of bread if desired.
Spread mayonnaise or tartar sauce on one side of each slice of bread.
Place a lettuce leaf on two slices of bread.
Place a salmon croquette on top of the lettuce on each slice.
Add sliced tomatoes and red onion on top of the croquettes.
Top with the remaining slices of bread to complete the sandwiches.

# Lime Coconut Smoothie Bowl

Ingredients:

For the Lime Coconut Smoothie Bowl:

2 large ripe bananas, frozen and sliced
1/2 cup coconut milk (canned, full-fat)
Zest and juice of 1 lime
1/2 cup plain Greek yogurt
1 tablespoon honey or maple syrup
(adjust to taste)
1/2 teaspoon vanilla extract

Toppings:

Sliced fresh kiwi
Toasted coconut flakes
Sliced almonds or other nuts
Chia seeds
Fresh mint leaves

Instructions:

Prepare the Lime Coconut Smoothie:
In a blender, combine the frozen banana slices, coconut milk, lime zest, lime juice, Greek yogurt, honey or maple syrup, and vanilla extract.
Blend on high until smooth and creamy. If the mixture is too thick, you can add a bit more coconut milk or a splash of water to reach your desired consistency.
Assemble the Smoothie Bowl:
Pour the lime coconut smoothie into two serving bowls.
Add Toppings:
Top each smoothie bowl with sliced kiwi, toasted coconut flakes, sliced almonds, chia seeds, and fresh mint leaves.
Serve:
Serve the lime coconut smoothie bowls immediately with a spoon.
Optional Customizations:
Feel free to get creative with additional toppings like fresh berries, granola, passion fruit, or even a drizzle of additional honey or maple syrup.
Enjoy your delicious and energizing Lime Coconut Smoothie Bowl, a perfect way to start your day with a burst of tropical flavors!

# Cheesy Vegetable Frittata

Ingredients:

4 large eggs
1/4 cup milk
Salt and pepper to taste
1 tablespoon olive oil
1/4 cup diced onion
1/4 cup diced bell peppers (any color)
1/4 cup diced zucchini
1/4 cup diced tomato
1/4 cup shredded cheddar cheese (or your preferred cheese)
2 tablespoons chopped fresh herbs (such as parsley, chives, or basil)

Instructions:

Preheat the Oven:
Preheat your oven's broiler on medium.
Prepare the Vegetables:
In an oven-safe skillet (about 8-10 inches in diameter), heat the olive oil over medium heat.
Add the diced onion, bell peppers, and zucchini. Sauté for about 2-3 minutes until the vegetables are slightly softened.
Whisk the Eggs:
In a bowl, whisk the eggs and milk together until well combined. Season with a pinch of salt and a dash of black pepper.
Add Tomatoes and Pour Eggs:
Add the diced tomatoes to the skillet with the sautéed vegetables.
Pour the whisked egg mixture over the sautéed vegetables and tomatoes.
Cook on the Stovetop:
Let the frittata cook on the stovetop for 3-4 minutes over medium heat, gently lifting the edges with a spatula to allow uncooked eggs to flow to the edges.
Add Cheese:
Sprinkle the shredded cheese evenly over the top of the frittata.
Broil in the Oven:
Transfer the skillet to the preheated oven's broiler. Make sure the skillet is oven-safe and the handle can withstand the heat.
Broil the frittata for about 3-4 minutes or until the top is set and slightly golden, and the cheese is melted and bubbly.
Garnish and Serve:
Carefully remove the skillet from the oven (remember, the handle will be hot!).
Sprinkle the chopped fresh herbs over the frittata.

# Oatmeal Pancakes

Ingredients:

1 cup old-fashioned rolled oats
1 cup milk (dairy or non-dairy)
1 large egg
2 tablespoons melted butter or oil
2 tablespoons honey or maple syrup
1 teaspoon vanilla extract
1/2 cup all-purpose flour
1 teaspoon baking powder
1/2 teaspoon baking soda
1/4 teaspoon salt
Cooking oil or butter for the pan

Instructions:

Prepare the Oatmeal:
In a mixing bowl, combine the oats and milk. Let them soak for about 10 minutes to soften the oats.

Prepare the Batter:
After the oats have soaked, add the egg, melted butter or oil, honey or maple syrup, and vanilla extract to the bowl. Mix well.

Combine Dry Ingredients:
In a separate bowl, whisk together the flour, baking powder, baking soda, and salt.

Mix Wet and Dry Ingredients:
Gradually add the dry ingredient mixture to the wet ingredients, stirring until just combined. Be careful not to overmix; a few lumps are okay.

Rest the Batter:
Let the batter rest for about 5-10 minutes. This helps the oats absorb some of the moisture and the batter to thicken slightly.

Cook the Pancakes:
Heat a skillet or griddle over medium heat. Add a small amount of cooking oil or butter to coat the surface.

Scoop and Cook:
Pour a small amount of batter (about 1/4 cup) onto the hot skillet for each pancake. Cook until bubbles form on the surface of the pancake and the edges look set. This usually takes about 2-3 minutes.

Flip and Finish Cooking:
Gently flip the pancakes with a spatula and cook for an additional 1-2 minutes, or until the other side is golden brown.

Repeat and Keep Warm:
Repeat the process with the remaining batter. You can keep the cooked pancakes warm in a low oven (around 200°F or 95°C) while you finish cooking the rest.

Serve:
Serve the oatmeal pancakes warm with your favorite toppings, such as fresh berries, sliced bananas, yogurt, nuts, or a drizzle of additional honey or maple syrup.

# Eggs Lorraine

Ingredients:

For the Eggs Lorraine: 4 slices of Canadian bacon or ham
2 English muffins, split and toasted
4 large eggs
1 tablespoon white vinegar (for poaching)
Salt and pepper to taste
Chopped fresh chives or parsley for garnish

For the Hollandaise Sauce:
2 large egg yolks
1 teaspoon lemon juice
1/2 cup unsalted butter, melted
Pinch of cayenne pepper
Salt to taste

Instructions:

Prepare the Hollandaise Sauce:
In a blender, combine the egg yolks and lemon juice. Blend for a few seconds until the mixture is smooth.
While the blender is running, slowly pour in the melted butter in a thin stream until the sauce is thickened and emulsified.
Add a pinch of cayenne pepper and salt to taste. Blend again to combine. Keep the sauce warm.
Poach the Eggs:
Fill a wide saucepan with about 2-3 inches of water. Add the white vinegar and bring the water to a gentle simmer.
Crack each egg into a small bowl. Create a gentle whirlpool in the simmering water using a spoon.
Slide one egg into the center of the whirlpool. Repeat with the remaining eggs, one at a time.
Allow the eggs to poach for about 3-4 minutes for a runny yolk, or longer if you prefer a firmer yolk. Use a slotted spoon to carefully remove the poached eggs from the water.
Prepare the Canadian Bacon (or Ham):
In a skillet, heat the Canadian bacon or ham slices until warmed through.
Assemble the Eggs Lorraine:
Place a toasted English muffin half on each plate.
Top each muffin half with a slice of Canadian bacon or ham.
Add Poached Eggs:
Gently place a poached egg on top of each bacon-covered muffin half.
Pour on Hollandaise Sauce:
Spoon a generous amount of the prepared Hollandaise sauce over each poached egg.
Garnish and Serve:
Sprinkle chopped fresh chives or parsley over the top for a burst of color and flavor.

# Apple Pancakes with Cider Syrup

Ingredients:

For the Apple Pancakes:

1 cup all-purpose flour
1 tablespoon granulated sugar
1 teaspoon baking powder
1/2 teaspoon baking soda
1/4 teaspoon salt
1/2 teaspoon ground cinnamon
1/2 cup buttermilk
1/2 cup apple cider
1 large egg
2 tablespoons unsalted butter, melted
1 medium apple, peeled, cored, and diced

For the Cider Syrup:

1/2 cup apple cider
1/4 cup pure maple syrup
1/2 teaspoon cornstarch (optional, for thickening)
1/2 teaspoon vanilla extract

Instructions:

Prepare the Cider Syrup:
In a small saucepan, combine the apple cider, maple syrup, and cornstarch (if using). Stir until the cornstarch is dissolved.
Place the saucepan over medium heat and bring the mixture to a gentle simmer.
Simmer for about 5-7 minutes, or until the syrup slightly thickens.
Remove the saucepan from the heat and stir in the vanilla extract. Set the syrup aside.
Prepare the Apple Pancake Batter:
In a mixing bowl, whisk together the flour, sugar, baking powder, baking soda, salt, and ground cinnamon.
In another bowl, whisk together the buttermilk, apple cider, egg, and melted butter.
Gradually add the wet ingredients to the dry ingredients, stirring until just combined.
Don't overmix; a few lumps are okay.
Gently fold in the diced apple.
Cook the Pancakes:
Heat a skillet or griddle over medium heat and lightly grease it with cooking spray or butter.
Pour about 1/4 cup of the pancake batter onto the skillet for each pancake. Use the back of a spoon to spread the batter into a round shape.
Flip and Finish Cooking:
Cook the pancakes for about 2-3 minutes on the first side, or until bubbles form on the surface and the edges look set.
Carefully flip the pancakes with a spatula and cook for an additional 1-2 minutes, or until the other side is golden brown.

# Bacon-Broccoli Quiche Cups

Ingredients:

2 sheets of pre-made pie crust (or make your own)
4 strips of bacon, cooked and crumbled
1/2 cup broccoli florets, blanched and chopped
1/2 cup shredded cheddar cheese (or your preferred cheese)
3 large eggs
1/2 cup milk (dairy or non-dairy)
Salt and pepper to taste
Pinch of nutmeg (optional)
Chopped fresh chives or parsley for garnish (optional)

Instructions:

Preheat the Oven:
Preheat your oven to 375°F (190°C).
Prepare the Pie Crust:
Roll out the pie crusts and use a round cutter to cut out circles that fit into the cups of a muffin tin.
Gently press each circle into the muffin cups, forming small crusts.
Add Fillings:
Divide the crumbled bacon and chopped broccoli evenly among the pie crusts.
Add Cheese:
Sprinkle shredded cheddar cheese over the bacon and broccoli in each cup.
Prepare the Egg Mixture:
In a bowl, whisk together the eggs, milk, salt, pepper, and a pinch of nutmeg if using.
Pour the Egg Mixture:
Carefully pour the egg mixture into each muffin cup, filling them about 3/4 full.
Bake:
Place the muffin tin in the preheated oven and bake for about 18-20 minutes, or until the quiche cups are set and the edges are golden brown.
Cool and Garnish:
Allow the quiche cups to cool slightly before removing them from the muffin tin.
If desired, garnish with chopped fresh chives or parsley.
Serve:
Serve the Bacon-Broccoli Quiche Cups warm as a delightful breakfast or brunch for two.

# Creamy Chicken Rice Soup

Ingredients:

1 tablespoon butter
1/4 cup diced onion
1/4 cup diced carrots
1/4 cup diced celery
1 garlic clove, minced
2 cups chicken broth
1 cup cooked chicken breast, shredded
1/2 cup cooked white rice
1/2 cup heavy cream
Salt and pepper to taste
Chopped fresh parsley for garnish
(optional)

Instructions:

Sauté Vegetables:
In a medium pot, melt the butter over medium heat.
Add the diced onion, carrots, and celery. Sauté for about 3-4 minutes until the vegetables start to soften.
Add Garlic:
Add the minced garlic to the pot and sauté for another 1 minute until fragrant.
Add Chicken Broth:
Pour in the chicken broth, and bring the mixture to a simmer. Let it cook for about 10 minutes, allowing the flavors to meld.
Add Chicken and Rice:
Add the shredded cooked chicken breast and cooked white rice to the pot. Stir to combine.
Add Cream:
Pour in the heavy cream and stir to incorporate. Let the soup simmer for another 5-7 minutes.
Season:
Taste the soup and season with salt and pepper as needed. Remember that the chicken broth might already have salt, so adjust accordingly.
Serve:
Ladle the creamy chicken rice soup into bowls.
Garnish:
If desired, garnish with chopped fresh parsley for a pop of color and freshness.
Enjoy:
Serve the soup warm and savor the comforting flavors.

# Vegetable Turkey Soup

Ingredients:

1 tablespoon olive oil
1/2 cup diced onion
1/2 cup diced carrots
1/2 cup diced celery
1 garlic clove, minced
4 cups turkey or chicken broth
1 cup cooked turkey, shredded or diced
1 cup mixed vegetables (frozen or fresh), such as peas, corn, and green beans
1 bay leaf
1/2 teaspoon dried thyme
Salt and pepper to taste
Chopped fresh parsley for garnish (optional)

Instructions:

Sauté Vegetables:
In a medium pot, heat the olive oil over medium heat.
Add the diced onion, carrots, and celery. Sauté for about 3-4 minutes until the vegetables start to soften.
Add Garlic:
Add the minced garlic to the pot and sauté for another 1 minute until fragrant.
Add Broth:
Pour in the turkey or chicken broth, and bring the mixture to a simmer. Let it cook for about 10 minutes, allowing the flavors to meld.
Add Turkey and Vegetables:
Add the cooked turkey and mixed vegetables to the pot. Stir to combine.
Season and Add Herbs:
Drop in the bay leaf and add the dried thyme.
Season the soup with salt and pepper to taste.
Simmer:
Let the soup simmer for another 10-15 minutes, allowing the flavors to develop and the vegetables to become tender.
Taste and Adjust:
Taste the soup and adjust the seasonings as needed.
Remove Bay Leaf:
Remove the bay leaf from the soup and discard.
Serve:
Ladle the vegetable turkey soup into bowls.
Garnish:
If desired, garnish with chopped fresh parsley for a burst of color and flavor.
Enjoy:
Serve the soup warm and enjoy the wholesome flavors.
This Vegetable Turkey Soup is a great way to use leftover turkey and create a nutritious and comforting meal for two. Feel free to customize the vegetables and herbs to your liking.

# Vegan Carrot Soup

Ingredients:

1 tablespoon olive oil
1/2 cup diced onion
2 cups carrots, peeled and chopped
1 small potato, peeled and chopped (for creaminess)
1 garlic clove, minced
3 cups vegetable broth
1/2 teaspoon ground cumin
1/4 teaspoon ground turmeric
1/4 teaspoon ground ginger
Salt and pepper to taste
1/2 cup coconut milk (canned, full-fat)
Fresh cilantro or parsley for garnish (optional)
Toasted pumpkin seeds for crunch (optional)

Instructions:

Sauté Vegetables:
In a medium pot, heat the olive oil over medium heat.
Add the diced onion and sauté for about 2-3 minutes until it becomes translucent.
Add Carrots and Potato:
Add the chopped carrots and potato to the pot. Sauté for another 3-4 minutes, stirring occasionally.
Add Garlic and Spices:
Add the minced garlic, ground cumin, ground turmeric, and ground ginger. Sauté for about 1 minute until fragrant.
Add Vegetable Broth:
Pour in the vegetable broth and bring the mixture to a simmer.
Simmer and Cook:
Cover the pot and let the soup simmer for about 15-20 minutes, or until the carrots and potato are tender and cooked through.
Blend the Soup:
Using an immersion blender or regular blender (in batches if necessary), blend the soup until smooth and creamy.
Season and Add Coconut Milk:
Return the blended soup to the pot over low heat.
Season with salt and pepper to taste.
Stir in the coconut milk to add creaminess.
Heat Through:
Let the soup heat through, but avoid boiling it after adding the coconut milk.
Serve:
Ladle the vegan carrot soup into bowls.
Garnish:
If desired, garnish with fresh cilantro or parsley for a pop of freshness and color.
Toasted pumpkin seeds can be sprinkled on top for extra crunch.

# Reuben Sandwich

Ingredients:

4 slices of rye bread
1/2 lb (about 225g) deli-sliced corned beef
1/2 cup sauerkraut, drained
1/2 cup shredded Swiss cheese
1/4 cup Russian or Thousand Island dressing
2 tablespoons unsalted butter, softened

Instructions:

Preheat a Griddle or Skillet:
Preheat a griddle or large skillet over medium heat.
Assemble the Sandwiches:
Lay out the slices of rye bread.
On two of the slices, layer the deli-sliced corned beef, followed by the sauerkraut, and then the shredded Swiss cheese.
Spread Dressing:
Spread the Russian or Thousand Island dressing on the other two slices of rye bread.
Combine Sandwiches:
Place the dressed slices of bread on top of the cheese to complete the sandwiches.
Butter the Bread:
Spread softened butter on the outsides of the sandwiches. This will help achieve a crispy and golden-brown crust when cooking.
Cook the Sandwiches:
Place the assembled sandwiches on the preheated griddle or skillet.
Cook for about 3-4 minutes on each side, or until the bread is toasted and the cheese is melted.
Serve:
Carefully remove the Reuben sandwiches from the griddle or skillet.
Slice each sandwich in half diagonally and serve warm.

# Buffalo Chicken Wrap

Ingredients:

For the Buffalo Chicken:
1 cup cooked and shredded chicken breast (you can use rotisserie chicken)
2-3 tablespoons buffalo sauce (adjust to taste)
1 tablespoon melted butter
Salt and pepper to taste

For the Wraps:

2 large flour tortillas or wraps
1/2 cup shredded lettuce
1/4 cup diced tomatoes
1/4 cup diced celery
1/4 cup crumbled blue cheese (or your preferred cheese)
2 tablespoons ranch or blue cheese dressing

Instructions:

Prepare the Buffalo Chicken:
In a bowl, combine the shredded chicken with the buffalo sauce and melted butter.
Toss to coat the chicken evenly.
Season with salt and pepper to taste.
Prepare the Wraps:
Lay out the flour tortillas on a clean surface.
Assemble the Wraps:
Divide the shredded lettuce between the two tortillas, placing it in the center of each.
Add Buffalo Chicken:
Divide the buffalo chicken mixture and place it on top of the lettuce in each tortilla.
Add Toppings:
Sprinkle diced tomatoes, diced celery, and crumbled blue cheese over the buffalo chicken in each tortilla.
Drizzle Dressing:
Drizzle ranch or blue cheese dressing over the toppings in each tortilla.
Wrap the Wraps:
Fold in the sides of each tortilla and then roll them up tightly, enclosing the fillings.
Serve:
Cut each wrap in half diagonally and serve immediately.

# BBQ Tempeh Sandwiches

Ingredients:

For the BBQ Tempeh:
1 package (8 oz) tempeh, sliced into thin strips
1/2 cup barbecue sauce
2 tablespoons olive oil
2 cloves garlic, minced
1/2 teaspoon smoked paprika
Salt and pepper to taste

For the Sandwiches:

4 burger buns or rolls
1 cup coleslaw (store-bought or homemade)
Sliced red onion (optional)
Sliced pickles (optional)

Instructions:

Marinate the Tempeh:
In a bowl, whisk together the barbecue sauce, olive oil, minced garlic, smoked paprika, salt, and pepper.
Add the tempeh slices to the marinade and let them marinate for at least 15-20 minutes, or longer for more flavor.
Cook the Tempeh:
Heat a skillet over medium heat.
Add the marinated tempeh slices to the skillet and cook for about 3-4 minutes on each side, or until they are heated through and have a nice caramelized texture.
Assemble the Sandwiches:
Toast the burger buns or rolls if desired.
Build the Sandwiches:
Place a layer of coleslaw on the bottom half of each bun.
Top the coleslaw with a few slices of the cooked BBQ tempeh.
Add Toppings:
If desired, add sliced red onion and pickles on top of the tempeh.
Complete the Sandwiches:
Place the top half of the bun on each sandwich to complete them.
Serve:
Serve the BBQ Tempeh Sandwiches with some additional coleslaw and your favorite side dish.
Enjoy:
These BBQ Tempeh Sandwiches offer a hearty and flavorful vegan meal for two, perfect for lunch or dinner.

# Gyro Sandwich

Ingredients:

For the Gyro Meat:
1/2 lb (about 225g) ground lamb or beef (or a mixture)
1/2 teaspoon ground cumin
1/2 teaspoon ground coriander
1/2 teaspoon paprika
1/4 teaspoon garlic powder
Salt and pepper to taste

For the Tzatziki Sauce:

1/2 cup Greek yogurt
1/4 cup grated cucumber, squeezed to remove excess moisture
1 clove garlic, minced
1 tablespoon fresh lemon juice
1 tablespoon chopped fresh dill (or mint)
Salt and pepper to taste

For Assembling the Sandwiches:

2 pita breads or flatbreads
Sliced tomatoes
Sliced red onion
Sliced cucumber
Chopped fresh parsley
Optional: Crumbled feta cheese

Instructions:

Prepare the Tzatziki Sauce:
In a bowl, combine the Greek yogurt, grated cucumber, minced garlic, lemon juice, chopped fresh dill, salt, and pepper. Mix well and refrigerate while you prepare the rest of the ingredients.

Prepare the Gyro Meat:
In a mixing bowl, combine the ground lamb or beef with the ground cumin, ground coriander, paprika, garlic powder, salt, and pepper. Mix well to combine the spices with the meat.

Cook the Gyro Meat:
Heat a skillet over medium-high heat. Add the seasoned meat mixture and cook, breaking it up with a spatula, until it's browned and cooked through. Drain any excess fat.

Assemble the Gyro Sandwiches:
Warm the pita breads or flatbreads. You can do this in a toaster, oven, or on a stovetop skillet.

Layer the Fillings:
On each warmed pita, layer the cooked gyro meat, sliced tomatoes, sliced red onion, and sliced cucumber.

Add Tzatziki Sauce:
Drizzle a generous amount of tzatziki sauce over the fillings.

Garnish and Serve:
Sprinkle chopped fresh parsley on top of the fillings.
If desired, crumble some feta cheese over the top.

Fold and Serve:
Fold the pita over the fillings to form a sandwich.

Enjoy:
Serve the Gyro Sandwiches warm, and enjoy the flavors of this classic Greek dish!

# Steak Sandwich

Ingredients:
For the Steak:
2 small ribeye steaks (about 8 oz each)
Salt and pepper to taste
1 tablespoon olive oil
2 cloves garlic, minced
1 tablespoon fresh rosemary, chopped
(or your preferred herbs)

For Assembling the Sandwiches:
2 ciabatta rolls or your favorite bread, sliced and toasted
Sliced red onion
Sliced tomatoes
Arugula or lettuce
Optional: Sliced cheese (such as provolone or cheddar)
Optional: Steak sauce or horseradish sauce

Instructions:
Prepare the Steak:
Preheat a grill or skillet over high heat.
Rub the steaks with olive oil and season both sides with salt, pepper, and chopped fresh rosemary (or your preferred herbs).
Grill or sear the steaks for about 3-4 minutes on each side, or until they reach your desired level of doneness. Let them rest for a few minutes before slicing.
Slice the Steak:
After resting, slice the cooked steaks against the grain into thin strips.
Assemble the Sandwiches:
Lay out the sliced and toasted ciabatta rolls or bread slices.
Layer the Fillings:
On one side of each roll, layer the sliced steak, followed by sliced red onion, sliced tomatoes, and arugula or lettuce.
Add Cheese (Optional):
If desired, you can add a slice of cheese on top of the steak while it's still warm to allow it to melt slightly.
Add Sauce (Optional):
Drizzle with steak sauce or horseradish sauce, if you like.
Complete the Sandwiches:
Place the other half of the ciabatta rolls on top to complete the sandwiches.
Serve:
Serve the Steak Sandwiches warm, and optionally, with a side of fries or a salad.
Enjoy:
Savor the deliciousness of a perfectly cooked steak sandwich!

# Cuban Sandwich

Ingredients:

1 Cuban bread loaf or French baguette (about 12 inches long)
4 slices of cooked ham
4 slices of roast pork (leftover or deli-sliced)
4 slices of Swiss cheese
8 dill pickle slices
Yellow mustard
Butter or margarine, softened

Instructions:

Prepare the Bread:
If using a whole Cuban bread loaf, slice it in half lengthwise to create the top and bottom of the sandwich.
Assemble the Cuban Sandwiches:
Lay out the bread pieces.
On the bottom half of the bread, spread a thin layer of yellow mustard.
Layer the Fillings:
Place a layer of cooked ham on top of the mustard.
Next, add the roast pork slices.
Add Pickles and Cheese:
Lay the dill pickle slices evenly over the roast pork.
Top the pickles with slices of Swiss cheese.
Complete the Sandwiches:
Place the top half of the bread over the cheese to complete the sandwiches.
Butter the Bread:
Spread softened butter or margarine on the outside of the bread on both the top and bottom halves of the sandwiches.
Cook the Sandwiches:
Heat a skillet or panini press over medium heat.
Place the Cuban sandwiches in the skillet or press.
Use a heavy pan or a press to weigh down the sandwiches slightly as they cook.
Grill and Press:
Cook the sandwiches for about 3-4 minutes on each side, or until the bread is toasted and the cheese is melted.

# Ham Sandwich

Ingredients:

4 slices of your favorite bread (such as whole wheat, sourdough, or multigrain)
6-8 slices of cooked ham
4 lettuce leaves
2-4 slices of tomato
4 slices of cheese (cheddar, Swiss, or your choice)
Mayonnaise or mustard (optional)
Salt and pepper to taste

Instructions:

Prepare the Bread:
Lay out the four slices of bread on a clean surface.
Layer the Ingredients:
On two of the bread slices, lay down a lettuce leaf.
Top the lettuce with 3-4 slices of cooked ham on each sandwich.
Add Cheese and Tomato:
Lay slices of cheese over the ham on each sandwich.
Place 1-2 slices of tomato on each sandwich.
Add Condiments (Optional):
Spread a thin layer of mayonnaise or mustard on the remaining two slices of bread, if desired.
Complete the Sandwiches:
Place the bread slices with condiments on top of the cheese and tomato to complete the sandwiches.
Serve:
Serve the Ham Sandwiches as is, or cut them in half diagonally for easier handling.
Enjoy:
Enjoy your classic Ham Sandwiches as a quick and satisfying lunch or snack for two.

# Italian Chopped Salad

Ingredients:

For the Salad:

4 cups chopped Romaine lettuce
1 cup chopped cucumber
1 cup chopped tomatoes
1/2 cup chopped red onion
1/2 cup chopped bell peppers (mix of colors)
1/2 cup chopped black olives
1/2 cup chopped pepperoni or salami
1/2 cup shredded mozzarella cheese
1/4 cup chopped fresh basil
1/4 cup chopped fresh parsley

For the Italian Vinaigrette:

3 tablespoons extra-virgin olive oil
1 tablespoon red wine vinegar
1 teaspoon Dijon mustard
1 clove garlic, minced
1/2 teaspoon dried oregano
Salt and pepper to taste

Instructions:

Prepare the Salad:
In a large salad bowl, combine the chopped Romaine lettuce, cucumber, tomatoes, red onion, bell peppers, black olives, pepperoni or salami, shredded mozzarella cheese, chopped fresh basil, and chopped fresh parsley.
Prepare the Italian Vinaigrette:
In a small bowl, whisk together the extra-virgin olive oil, red wine vinegar, Dijon mustard, minced garlic, dried oregano, salt, and pepper until well combined.
Dress the Salad:
Drizzle the Italian vinaigrette over the salad.
Toss the Salad:
Gently toss all the ingredients together to coat them with the vinaigrette and distribute the flavors.
Serve:
Divide the Italian Chopped Salad between two serving plates or bowls.
Enjoy:
Serve the salad as a refreshing and flavorful meal for two. Optionally, you can serve it with some crusty bread or a side of your choice.
This Italian Chopped Salad is packed with a variety of fresh and vibrant ingredients, and the homemade vinaigrette brings all the flavors together. It's perfect for a light and satisfying lunch or dinner.

# Homemade Caesar Salad

Ingredients:
For the Caesar Salad:
1 large head of Romaine lettuce, washed and torn into bite-sized pieces
1/2 cup croutons (store-bought or homemade)
1/4 cup grated Parmesan cheese

For the Caesar Dressing:
1/4 cup mayonnaise
2 tablespoons grated Parmesan cheese
2 tablespoons freshly squeezed lemon juice
1 tablespoon Dijon mustard
1 garlic clove, minced
2 anchovy fillets, minced (optional)
2 tablespoons olive oil
Salt and freshly ground black pepper, to taste

Instructions:

Prepare the Caesar Dressing:
In a bowl, whisk together the mayonnaise, grated Parmesan cheese, lemon juice, Dijon mustard, minced garlic, and minced anchovy fillets (if using).
Emulsify the Dressing:
While whisking continuously, slowly drizzle in the olive oil until the dressing is well combined and slightly thickened.
Season with salt and freshly ground black pepper to taste. Adjust the amounts of lemon juice and salt to achieve your preferred flavor balance.
Assemble the Caesar Salad:
In a large salad bowl, add the torn Romaine lettuce.
Add Croutons:
Sprinkle the croutons over the lettuce.
Drizzle with Dressing:
Drizzle a portion of the Caesar dressing over the salad. Start with a small amount and add more as needed, tossing gently to coat the lettuce and croutons.
Toss the Salad:
Gently toss the ingredients to evenly distribute the dressing.
Serve:
Divide the dressed Caesar Salad between two serving plates or bowls.
Garnish with Cheese:
Sprinkle grated Parmesan cheese over the top of each salad.
Enjoy:

# Beet Salad

Ingredients:
For the Salad:
2 medium-sized beets, roasted, peeled, and sliced
4 cups mixed salad greens (such as arugula, spinach, or mixed baby greens)
1/4 cup crumbled goat cheese or feta cheese
1/4 cup chopped walnuts or pecans, toasted
1/4 cup thinly sliced red onion
Fresh herbs for garnish (such as parsley or dill)

For the Balsamic Vinaigrette:

3 tablespoons extra-virgin olive oil
1 tablespoon balsamic vinegar
1 teaspoon Dijon mustard
1 teaspoon honey or maple syrup (optional)
Salt and freshly ground black pepper, to taste

Instructions:

Prepare the Roasted Beets:
Preheat the oven to 400°F (200°C).
Wash and trim the beets, leaving about an inch of the stem. Wrap each beet in aluminum foil and place them on a baking sheet.
Roast the beets in the preheated oven for about 45-60 minutes, or until they are tender when pierced with a fork.
Let the roasted beets cool, then peel them and slice them into thin rounds.
Prepare the Balsamic Vinaigrette:
In a small bowl, whisk together the extra-virgin olive oil, balsamic vinegar, Dijon mustard, honey or maple syrup (if using), salt, and freshly ground black pepper until well combined.
Assemble the Beet Salad:
On two serving plates, arrange a bed of mixed salad greens.
Add Roasted Beets:
Arrange the sliced roasted beets over the salad greens.
Add Cheese, Nuts, and Onion:
Sprinkle crumbled goat cheese or feta cheese, toasted walnuts or pecans, and thinly sliced red onion over the beets.
Drizzle with Dressing:
Drizzle the balsamic vinaigrette over the salad.
Garnish:
Garnish the salad with fresh herbs, such as chopped parsley or dill.
Enjoy:
Serve the Beet Salad as a delightful and nutritious appetizer or main course for two.

# Marinated Chickpea and Feta Salad

Ingredients:

For the Salad:
1 can (15 oz) chickpeas, drained and rinsed
1 cup cherry tomatoes, halved
1/2 cucumber, diced
1/4 red onion, finely chopped
1/4 cup crumbled feta cheese
2 tablespoons chopped fresh parsley

For the Marinade:
3 tablespoons extra-virgin olive oil
2 tablespoons lemon juice
1 garlic clove, minced
1/2 teaspoon dried oregano
Salt and pepper to taste

Instructions:

In a medium bowl, whisk together the olive oil, lemon juice, minced garlic, dried oregano, salt, and pepper to create the marinade.
Add the drained and rinsed chickpeas to the marinade. Stir gently to coat the chickpeas in the marinade. Let them marinate for about 15-20 minutes to soak up the flavors.
In a separate mixing bowl, combine the halved cherry tomatoes, diced cucumber, chopped red onion, and crumbled feta cheese.
After the chickpeas have marinated, add them to the bowl with the vegetables and feta cheese. Toss everything together gently to combine.
Sprinkle the chopped fresh parsley over the salad for added freshness and color.
Taste and adjust the seasoning, adding more salt, pepper, or lemon juice if needed.
Let the salad sit for a few minutes to allow the flavors to meld together.
Serve the marinated chickpea and feta salad in individual bowls. You can enjoy it as a light lunch, a side dish, or even as a main course.
This Marinated Chickpea and Feta Salad is not only delicious but also packed with protein and nutrients. It's a perfect choice for a quick and healthy meal for two!

# Vegetarian Kale Taco Salad

Ingredients:

For the Salad:
4 cups kale, stems removed and chopped
1 cup canned black beans, drained and rinsed
1 cup corn kernels (fresh, frozen, or canned)
1 avocado, diced
1/2 cup cherry tomatoes, halved
1/4 cup red onion, finely chopped
1/4 cup shredded cheddar cheese (optional)
1/4 cup crushed tortilla chips

For the Taco Seasoning:
1 teaspoon chili powder
1/2 teaspoon cumin
1/4 teaspoon paprika
1/4 teaspoon garlic powder
1/4 teaspoon onion powder
1/8 teaspoon cayenne pepper (adjust to taste)
Salt and pepper to taste

For the Lime-Cilantro Dressing:

1/4 cup plain Greek yogurt
2 tablespoons lime juice
2 tablespoons chopped fresh cilantro
Salt and pepper to taste

Instructions:

In a small bowl, mix together all the taco seasoning ingredients: chili powder, cumin, paprika, garlic powder, onion powder, cayenne pepper, salt, and pepper.
In a large mixing bowl, place the chopped kale. Drizzle a bit of olive oil over the kale and massage it with your hands for a few minutes until it becomes slightly softer and more tender.
Sprinkle the taco seasoning over the kale and toss to evenly coat the leaves with the seasoning.
Add the drained black beans, corn, diced avocado, halved cherry tomatoes, chopped red onion, and shredded cheddar cheese (if using) to the bowl with the seasoned kale.
In a separate small bowl, whisk together the Greek yogurt, lime juice, chopped cilantro, salt, and pepper to create the lime-cilantro dressing.
Drizzle the lime-cilantro dressing over the salad and toss everything together to combine.
Divide the salad between two serving plates or bowls.
Top the salad with crushed tortilla chips for a crunchy texture.
Serve the Vegetarian Kale Taco Salad immediately, and you can optionally offer extra lime wedges and cilantro for garnish.

# Mussels with Harissa and Basil

Ingredients:

1 pound (450g) fresh mussels, cleaned and debearded
2 tablespoons olive oil
2 cloves garlic, minced
1 tablespoon harissa paste (adjust to taste for spice level)
1/2 cup dry white wine
1/4 cup chopped fresh basil
Salt and pepper to taste
Crusty bread, for serving

Instructions:

Prepare the Mussels:
Scrub and clean the mussels under cold water, removing any dirt and the "beard" (the stringy bit protruding from the shell).
Discard any mussels that are open and do not close when tapped on a hard surface.
Cook the Mussels:
In a large pot or deep skillet with a lid, heat the olive oil over medium heat.
Add the minced garlic and sauté for about 1 minute until fragrant, taking care not to let it brown.
Add Harissa and Wine:
Stir in the harissa paste, coating the garlic with the paste.
Pour in the dry white wine and let it simmer for a minute to slightly reduce and meld the flavors.
Add Mussels and Basil:
Add the cleaned mussels to the pot.
Cover the pot with a lid and let the mussels cook for about 5-7 minutes, shaking the pot occasionally, until the mussels have opened. Discard any mussels that do not open.
Season and Serve:
Once the mussels are cooked and their shells have opened, season with a pinch of salt and a bit of freshly ground black pepper to taste.
Stir in the chopped fresh basil.
Serve:
Divide the mussels and broth between two serving bowls.
Serve the mussels with crusty bread on the side for dipping into the flavorful broth.
Enjoy:
Enjoy the Mussels with Harissa and Basil immediately while they're still hot. Use the bread to soak up the delicious broth.
This Mussels with Harissa and Basil recipe brings together the rich flavors of mussels, the heat of harissa, and the aromatic freshness of basil. It's a wonderful dish for a cozy dinner for two, perfect for enjoying with a glass of wine and good company.

# Venetian Shrimp with Polenta

Ingredients:

For the Shrimp:
12 large shrimp, peeled and deveined
2 tablespoons olive oil
2 cloves garlic, minced
1/4 teaspoon red pepper flakes (adjust to taste)
1/4 cup dry white wine
1/2 cup diced tomatoes (canned or fresh)
2 tablespoons chopped fresh parsley
Salt and pepper to taste

For the Polenta:
1/2 cup polenta (cornmeal)
2 cups water
Salt to taste
2 tablespoons butter
1/4 cup grated Parmesan cheese

Instructions:

Prepare the Shrimp:
In a skillet, heat the olive oil over medium heat.
Add the minced garlic and red pepper flakes. Sauté for about 1 minute until fragrant, being careful not to let the garlic burn.
Add the shrimp to the skillet and cook for about 2 minutes on each side until they turn pink and opaque.
Pour in the white wine and let it simmer for a minute to reduce slightly.
Add the diced tomatoes to the skillet and let everything simmer together for another 2-3 minutes.
Season with salt and pepper to taste. Stir in the chopped parsley.

Prepare the Polenta:
In a medium saucepan, bring 2 cups of water to a boil. Add a pinch of salt.
Gradually whisk in the polenta, stirring constantly to prevent lumps from forming.
Reduce the heat to low and continue to cook the polenta, stirring frequently, for about 15-20 minutes until it thickens and becomes creamy.
Stir in the butter and grated Parmesan cheese until well incorporated. Season with additional salt if needed.

# Spaghetti with Clams and Garlic

Ingredients:

8 oz (about 225g) spaghetti
1 pound (450g) fresh clams (such as Manila or littleneck), scrubbed and cleaned
4 tablespoons olive oil
3 cloves garlic, thinly sliced
1/4 teaspoon red pepper flakes (adjust to taste)
1/4 cup dry white wine
2 tablespoons chopped fresh parsley
Salt and black pepper to taste

Instructions:

Prepare the Clams:
Scrub the clams under cold water to remove any dirt or sand.
Discard any clams that are cracked or do not close when tapped.
Cook the Spaghetti:
In a large pot of salted boiling water, cook the spaghetti according to the package instructions until al dente. Drain and set aside.
Cook the Clams and Sauce:
In a large skillet or pan, heat 2 tablespoons of olive oil over medium heat.
Add the sliced garlic and red pepper flakes. Sauté for about 1 minute until the garlic is fragrant and just starting to turn golden. Be careful not to let it burn.
Add the Clams:
Increase the heat to medium-high.
Add the cleaned clams to the skillet.
Pour in the white wine and cover the skillet with a lid. Let the clams steam for about 5-7 minutes, or until they open. Discard any clams that do not open.
Combine Pasta and Clams:
Use a slotted spoon to transfer the cooked clams to a bowl, leaving the flavorful liquid in the skillet.
Finish the Dish:
Add the cooked spaghetti to the skillet with the reserved liquid.
Drizzle with the remaining 2 tablespoons of olive oil and toss the spaghetti to coat it in the garlic-infused liquid.
Assemble the Dish:
Divide the spaghetti and sauce between two serving plates.
Arrange the steamed clams over the spaghetti.
Garnish and Serve:
Sprinkle chopped fresh parsley over the dish for freshness and color.
Season with salt and black pepper to taste.
Enjoy:
Serve the Spaghetti with Clams and Garlic immediately while it's hot.

# Grilled Grouper

Ingredients:

2 grouper fillets (about 6-8 oz each)
2 tablespoons olive oil
2 tablespoons lemon juice
2 cloves garlic, minced
1 teaspoon dried oregano
1 teaspoon paprika
Salt and black pepper to taste
Lemon wedges and fresh parsley for garnish

Instructions:

Prepare the Marinade:
In a bowl, whisk together the olive oil, lemon juice, minced garlic, dried oregano, paprika, salt, and black pepper to create the marinade.
Marinate the Grouper:
Place the grouper fillets in a shallow dish or a resealable plastic bag.
Pour the marinade over the fillets, ensuring they are well coated. Marinate in the refrigerator for about 30 minutes to 1 hour, turning the fillets halfway through.
Preheat the Grill:
Preheat your grill to medium-high heat. Clean and oil the grill grates to prevent sticking.
Grill the Grouper:
Remove the fillets from the marinade and let any excess marinade drip off.
Place the fillets on the grill grates. Cook for about 4-5 minutes per side, depending on the thickness of the fillets. The grouper is done when it flakes easily with a fork and is opaque throughout.
Basting (Optional):
You can brush the fillets with any remaining marinade during grilling to enhance the flavor.
Serve:
Carefully remove the grilled grouper fillets from the grill and transfer them to serving plates.
Garnish and Enjoy:
Garnish the grilled grouper with lemon wedges and fresh parsley.
Serve the grouper fillets with your choice of side dishes, such as rice, grilled vegetables, or a fresh salad.
Grilled grouper is a versatile dish that pairs well with a variety of flavors. The combination of the marinade's citrus and herbs along with the smoky grill marks makes for a wonderful dining experience. Enjoy your delicious grilled grouper meal!

# Fried Oysters with Remoulade

Ingredients:

For the Fried Oysters:
12 fresh oysters, shucked and drained
1/2 cup all-purpose flour
1/2 cup cornmeal
1 teaspoon Old Bay seasoning (or your favorite seafood seasoning)
Salt and black pepper to taste
Vegetable oil, for frying

For the Remoulade Sauce:
1/4 cup mayonnaise
1 tablespoon Dijon mustard
1 tablespoon chopped fresh parsley
1 tablespoon chopped green onion or chives
1 tablespoon capers, chopped
1 teaspoon lemon juice
1 teaspoon Worcestershire sauce
1/2 teaspoon hot sauce (adjust to taste)
Salt and black pepper to taste

Instructions:

Prepare the Remoulade Sauce:
In a bowl, whisk together the mayonnaise, Dijon mustard, chopped parsley, chopped green onion, capers, lemon juice, Worcestershire sauce, and hot sauce.
Season the remoulade sauce with salt and black pepper to taste. Adjust the hot sauce to your preferred level of spiciness.
Cover the sauce and refrigerate it until you're ready to serve the fried oysters.
In a heavy-bottomed skillet or deep fryer, heat vegetable oil to 350°F (175°C).
In a shallow dish, mix together the all-purpose flour, cornmeal, Old Bay seasoning, salt, and black pepper.
Dredge each shucked oyster in the flour mixture, shaking off any excess.
Carefully place the coated oysters into the hot oil using tongs. Fry for about 2-3 minutes until they are golden brown and crispy. Be sure not to overcrowd the skillet - fry in batches if needed.
Once the oysters are fried, use a slotted spoon to transfer them to a plate lined with paper towels to drain any excess oil.
Arrange the fried oysters on a serving platter.
Serve the remoulade sauce alongside the fried oysters for dipping.
You can also garnish the dish with additional chopped parsley or lemon wedges.

# Tuna Croquettes

Ingredients:

For the Tuna Croquettes:
1 can (6-7 oz) canned tuna, drained and flaked
1/2 cup breadcrumbs
1/4 cup finely chopped onion
1/4 cup finely chopped celery
1/4 cup finely chopped bell pepper (any color)
1/4 cup mayonnaise
1 tablespoon Dijon mustard
1 tablespoon chopped fresh parsley
1 teaspoon lemon juice
1/2 teaspoon garlic powder
Salt and black pepper to taste
1/4 cup all-purpose flour (for coating)
1 egg, beaten (for coating)
Vegetable oil, for frying

For the Lemon-Dill Sauce:

1/4 cup mayonnaise
1 tablespoon lemon juice
1 teaspoon chopped fresh dill
Salt and black pepper to taste

Instructions:

Prepare the Tuna Croquettes:
In a bowl, combine the drained and flaked canned tuna, breadcrumbs, chopped onion, chopped celery, chopped bell pepper, mayonnaise, Dijon mustard, chopped parsley, lemon juice, garlic powder, salt, and black pepper.
Mix the ingredients until well combined. The mixture should hold together when shaped.
Divide the mixture into 4 equal portions and shape each portion into a patty.
Place the flour, beaten egg, and additional breadcrumbs in separate shallow dishes for coating.
Coat each tuna patty first in flour, then dip it in the beaten egg, and finally coat it with breadcrumbs, pressing gently to adhere.
Heat vegetable oil in a skillet over medium heat. Carefully add the coated tuna patties to the skillet.
Cook the croquettes for about 3-4 minutes on each side, or until they are golden brown and heated through.
Once cooked, transfer the croquettes to a plate lined with paper towels to drain any excess oil.
Prepare the Lemon-Dill Sauce:
In a small bowl, whisk together the mayonnaise, lemon juice, chopped dill, salt, and black pepper to create the sauce.

# Creamy Tuscan Chicken

Ingredients:

2 boneless, skinless chicken breasts
Salt and black pepper to taste
2 tablespoons olive oil, divided
3 cloves garlic, minced
1/4 teaspoon red pepper flakes (adjust to taste)
1/3 cup sun-dried tomatoes, chopped
1/2 cup chicken broth
1/2 cup heavy cream
1 cup fresh baby spinach
1 teaspoon dried Italian herbs (such as thyme, rosemary, oregano)
Grated Parmesan cheese for garnish
Chopped fresh parsley for garnish

Instructions:

Prepare the Chicken:
Season the chicken breasts with salt and black pepper on both sides.
In a large skillet, heat 1 tablespoon of olive oil over medium-high heat.
Add the chicken breasts and cook for about 4-5 minutes on each side, or until they are golden brown and cooked through. The internal temperature should reach 165°F (74°C).
Once cooked, remove the chicken from the skillet and set it aside on a plate.
In the same skillet, add the remaining 1 tablespoon of olive oil.
Add the minced garlic and red pepper flakes. Sauté for about 1 minute until fragrant.
Add Sun-Dried Tomatoes and Spinach:
Stir in the chopped sun-dried tomatoes and cook for another minute.
Pour in the chicken broth and scrape up any browned bits from the bottom of the skillet.
Reduce the heat to medium-low and pour in the heavy cream. Let the mixture simmer and thicken for a few minutes.
Add Spinach and Herbs:
Stir in the fresh baby spinach and dried Italian herbs. Allow the spinach to wilt in the sauce.
Return the cooked chicken breasts to the skillet, nestling them into the creamy sauce.
Simmer and Serve:
Let the chicken simmer in the sauce for a couple of minutes to heat through and absorb the flavors.
Sprinkle grated Parmesan cheese and chopped fresh parsley over the chicken and sauce before serving.
Serve the Creamy Tuscan Chicken over pasta, rice, or with crusty bread on the side. The creamy sauce, tangy sun-dried tomatoes, and vibrant spinach create a delightful and satisfying dish for a romantic dinner for two.

# Classic Stuffed Peppers

Ingredients:

2 large bell peppers (any color)
1/2 cup cooked rice (white or brown)
1/2 pound ground beef
1/4 cup diced onion
1/4 cup diced tomatoes
1/4 cup grated cheddar cheese (plus extra for topping)
1/4 cup tomato sauce
1 teaspoon Worcestershire sauce
1/2 teaspoon garlic powder
Salt and black pepper to taste

Instructions:

Preheat the Oven:
Preheat your oven to 375°F (190°C).
Prepare the Bell Peppers:
Cut the tops off the bell peppers and remove the seeds and membranes.
Place the bell peppers in a baking dish, standing upright.
Prepare the Filling:
In a skillet, brown the ground beef over medium heat. Drain any excess fat.
Add diced onion and cook until it's translucent.
Stir in the diced tomatoes, cooked rice, grated cheddar cheese, tomato sauce, Worcestershire sauce, garlic powder, salt, and black pepper. Mix well.
Stuff the Peppers:
Stuff the prepared bell peppers with the filling mixture.
Bake:
Place the stuffed peppers in the baking dish.
Top each pepper with additional grated cheddar cheese.
Bake:
Cover the baking dish with aluminum foil and bake in the preheated oven for about 25-30 minutes, or until the peppers are tender.
Serve:
Carefully remove the stuffed peppers from the oven.
Serve the stuffed peppers while they're hot.

# Classic Meatloaf

Ingredients:

For the Meatloaf:

1/2 pound ground beef
1/2 pound ground pork or ground veal (or use more ground beef)
1/2 cup breadcrumbs
1/4 cup milk
1/4 cup finely chopped onion
1/4 cup finely chopped bell pepper
1/4 cup finely chopped celery
1 large egg
2 tablespoons ketchup
1 teaspoon Worcestershire sauce
1 teaspoon dried thyme
1/2 teaspoon garlic powder
1/2 teaspoon salt
1/4 teaspoon black pepper

For the Topping:

1/4 cup ketchup
1 tablespoon brown sugar
1 tablespoon Dijon mustard

Instructions:

Preheat the Oven:
Preheat your oven to 350°F (175°C).
Prepare the Meatloaf Mixture:
In a large mixing bowl, combine the ground beef, ground pork or veal, breadcrumbs, milk, chopped onion, chopped bell pepper, chopped celery, egg, ketchup, Worcestershire sauce, dried thyme, garlic powder, salt, and black pepper.
Mix the Ingredients:
Gently mix the ingredients with your hands until well combined. Be careful not to overmix, as this can make the meatloaf dense.
Shape the Meatloaf:
Shape the meatloaf mixture into a loaf shape and place it in a baking dish.
Prepare the Topping:
In a small bowl, mix together ketchup, brown sugar, and Dijon mustard to create the topping sauce.
Add the Topping:
Spread the topping sauce over the top of the meatloaf, covering it evenly.
Bake:
Place the baking dish in the preheated oven and bake for about 45-55 minutes, or until the meatloaf is cooked through and reaches an internal temperature of 160°F (71°C).
Rest and Serve:
Remove the meatloaf from the oven and let it rest for a few minutes before slicing.
Slice and Serve:
Slice the meatloaf and serve it alongside your favorite sides, such as mashed potatoes and steamed vegetables.

# Air Fryer Pork Chops

Ingredients:

2 boneless pork chops (about 6-8 oz each)
1 tablespoon olive oil
1 teaspoon paprika
1/2 teaspoon garlic powder
1/2 teaspoon dried thyme
Salt and black pepper to taste

Instructions:

Preheat the Air Fryer:
Preheat your air fryer to 375°F (190°C) for a few minutes.

Season the Pork Chops:
In a small bowl, mix together the olive oil, paprika, garlic powder, dried thyme, salt, and black pepper to create a marinade.

Coat the Pork Chops:
Rub the pork chops with the prepared marinade, ensuring they are evenly coated.

Place in the Air Fryer:
Place the seasoned pork chops in a single layer in the air fryer basket. Make sure to leave some space between them for proper air circulation.

Air Fry:
Cook the pork chops in the air fryer for about 12-16 minutes, flipping them halfway through the cooking time. Cooking time can vary depending on the thickness of the pork chops and your air fryer model.

Check for Doneness:
Use a meat thermometer to check the internal temperature of the pork chops. They should reach an internal temperature of 145°F (63°C) for medium doneness. The temperature will continue to rise slightly as the pork chops rest.

Rest and Serve:
Once the pork chops are cooked to your desired doneness, remove them from the air fryer and let them rest for a few minutes before serving.

Serve:
Serve the air fryer pork chops with your favorite side dishes, such as roasted vegetables, potatoes, or a fresh salad.

# Spicy Salmon Bowl

Ingredients:

For the Spicy Salmon:
2 salmon fillets (about 6-8 oz each)
2 tablespoons soy sauce
1 tablespoon Sriracha sauce (adjust to taste)
1 tablespoon honey or maple syrup
1 tablespoon olive oil
1 teaspoon grated ginger
1 teaspoon minced garlic
Salt and black pepper to taste

For the Bowl:

1 cup cooked quinoa or rice
1 cup mixed vegetables (such as bell peppers, carrots, broccoli, etc.), chopped
1 avocado, sliced
1 tablespoon sesame seeds (optional)
Chopped green onions for garnish

For the Sauce:

2 tablespoons Greek yogurt or mayonnaise
1 tablespoon Sriracha sauce (adjust to taste)
1 teaspoon lime juice
Salt to taste

Instructions:

Prepare the Spicy Salmon:
In a bowl, whisk together the soy sauce, Sriracha sauce, honey or maple syrup, olive oil, grated ginger, minced garlic, salt, and black pepper.
Place the salmon fillets in a shallow dish and pour the marinade over them. Allow the salmon to marinate for about 15-30 minutes.
Preheat a skillet or grill pan over medium-high heat. Remove the salmon from the marinade and cook the fillets for about 4-5 minutes on each side, or until cooked through and flaky.
Prepare the Bowl:
Divide the cooked quinoa or rice between two serving bowls.
In the same skillet or grill pan, sauté the mixed vegetables until they're tender-crisp.
Place the sautéed vegetables, sliced avocado, and cooked salmon fillets on top of the quinoa or rice in the bowls.
Prepare the Sauce:
In a small bowl, mix together the Greek yogurt or mayonnaise, Sriracha sauce, lime juice, and a pinch of salt to create a creamy spicy sauce.
Assemble and Serve:
Drizzle the creamy spicy sauce over the salmon and vegetables in each bowl.
Sprinkle sesame seeds and chopped green onions over the bowls for added flavor and garnish.
Serve the Spicy Salmon Bowls immediately, and you can squeeze additional lime juice over the top if desired.

# Brick Chicken

Ingredients:

2 bone-in, skin-on chicken breasts
Salt and black pepper to taste
2 tablespoons olive oil
2 cloves garlic, minced
1 teaspoon dried rosemary (or other herbs of your choice)
1 lemon, sliced
Fresh herbs (such as thyme or parsley) for garnish

Instructions:

Prep the Chicken:
Pat the chicken breasts dry with paper towels. This helps to achieve crispy skin.
Season both sides of the chicken breasts with salt and black pepper.
Flavor the Olive Oil:
In a small bowl, mix together the olive oil, minced garlic, and dried rosemary.
Marinate the Chicken:
Rub the olive oil mixture all over the chicken breasts, ensuring they are well coated. Allow them to marinate for at least 15-30 minutes.
Preheat the Grill or Skillet:
Preheat a grill or a heavy skillet over medium-high heat. If using a skillet, you can also preheat the oven to 375°F (190°C).
Cook the Chicken:
Place the chicken breasts on the grill or in the preheated skillet, skin-side down. You can place a piece of parchment paper on top of the chicken to prevent direct contact with the weight.
If using a skillet, place a second heavy skillet or a clean brick wrapped in aluminum foil on top of the chicken to press it down.
Cook for about 7-8 minutes on the first side, until the skin is crispy and golden brown.
Flip and Continue Cooking:
Carefully remove the weight, flip the chicken breasts, and place the weight back on top.
Cook for another 7-8 minutes on the other side, until the chicken is cooked through and the internal temperature reaches 165°F (74°C).
Add Lemon Slices:
In the last couple of minutes of cooking, add lemon slices to the grill or skillet to char slightly and infuse flavor.
Rest and Serve:
Once cooked, remove the chicken from the grill or skillet and let it rest for a few minutes before slicing.
Garnish and Enjoy:
Garnish the chicken with fresh herbs and the charred lemon slices.
Serve the brick chicken with your choice of sides, such as roasted vegetables, potatoes, or a salad.

# Garlicky Lemon Baked Tilapia

Ingredients:

2 tilapia fillets (about 6-8 oz each)
2 tablespoons olive oil
2 cloves garlic, minced
Zest of 1 lemon
Juice of 1 lemon
1 teaspoon dried oregano
Salt and black pepper to taste
Chopped fresh parsley for garnish
Lemon slices for serving

Instructions:

Preheat the Oven:
Preheat your oven to 375°F (190°C).
Prepare the Marinade:
In a bowl, whisk together the olive oil, minced garlic, lemon zest, lemon juice, dried oregano, salt, and black pepper.
Marinate the Tilapia:
Place the tilapia fillets in a shallow dish or a resealable plastic bag.
Pour the marinade over the fillets and make sure they are well coated. Marinate for about 15-30 minutes.
Bake the Tilapia:
Line a baking dish with parchment paper or lightly grease it.
Place the marinated tilapia fillets in the baking dish.
Pour any remaining marinade over the fillets.
Bake in the Oven:
Bake the tilapia in the preheated oven for about 12-15 minutes, or until the fish flakes easily with a fork and is cooked through.
Garnish and Serve:
Once cooked, remove the tilapia from the oven and transfer the fillets to serving plates.
Garnish and Enjoy:
Garnish the baked tilapia with chopped fresh parsley.
Serve the tilapia with lemon slices on the side for an extra burst of flavor.
Serve with Sides:
Accompany the garlicky lemon baked tilapia with your choice of sides, such as steamed vegetables, rice, or a fresh salad.

# Snacks And Sides

# Best Banana Bread

Ingredients:

2 ripe bananas, mashed
1/4 cup granulated sugar
1/4 cup packed brown sugar
1/4 cup unsalted butter, melted
1 large egg
1/2 teaspoon vanilla extract
1 cup all-purpose flour
1/2 teaspoon baking soda
1/4 teaspoon salt
1/4 teaspoon ground cinnamon (optional)
1/4 cup chopped nuts (such as walnuts or pecans), optional

Instructions:

Preheat the Oven:
Preheat your oven to 350°F (175°C).
Grease a small loaf pan (approximately 6x3 inches) or line it with parchment paper.
Mix Wet Ingredients:
In a mixing bowl, combine the mashed bananas, granulated sugar, brown sugar, melted butter, egg, and vanilla extract. Mix well until everything is thoroughly combined.
Mix Dry Ingredients:
In a separate bowl, whisk together the flour, baking soda, salt, and ground cinnamon (if using).
Combine Wet and Dry Ingredients:
Gradually add the dry ingredients to the wet ingredients, stirring until just combined. Be careful not to overmix; a few lumps are okay.
Add Nuts (Optional):
If using chopped nuts, fold them into the batter.
Fill the Loaf Pan:
Pour the batter into the prepared loaf pan and spread it evenly.
Bake in the Oven:
Place the loaf pan in the preheated oven and bake for about 30-40 minutes, or until a toothpick inserted into the center of the bread comes out clean.
Cool and Serve:
Once baked, remove the banana bread from the oven and let it cool in the pan for about 10 minutes.
Carefully remove the bread from the pan and transfer it to a wire rack to cool completely.
Slice and Enjoy:
Once the banana bread has cooled, slice it into thick slices and enjoy!

# Easy Homemade Hummus

Ingredients:
1 can (15 oz) chickpeas (garbanzo beans), drained and rinsed
2 tablespoons tahini
2 tablespoons lemon juice
1 small garlic clove, minced
1/2 teaspoon ground cumin
Salt to taste
2-3 tablespoons olive oil
Water (as needed)
Paprika and chopped fresh parsley for garnish

Instructions:

Prepare the Chickpeas:
Drain and rinse the chickpeas thoroughly under cold water.
Combine Ingredients:

In a food processor, combine the chickpeas, tahini, lemon juice, minced garlic, ground cumin, and a pinch of salt.
Blend:
Pulse the ingredients in the food processor until the mixture is coarsely ground.
Add Olive Oil:
With the food processor running, gradually add the olive oil in a steady stream. Continue blending until the hummus becomes smooth and creamy.
Adjust Consistency:
If the hummus seems too thick, you can add a little water (start with 1 tablespoon) and blend again until you achieve the desired consistency.
Taste and Adjust Seasoning:
Taste the hummus and adjust the seasoning by adding more salt, lemon juice, or cumin if needed.
Serve:
Transfer the hummus to a serving dish.
Garnish:
Drizzle a little olive oil over the top of the hummus.
Sprinkle with paprika and chopped fresh parsley for added flavor and visual appeal.
Serve and Enjoy:
Serve the homemade hummus with pita bread, fresh vegetables, or your favorite dipping items.

# Instant Pot Baby Potatoes

Ingredients:

1 pound baby potatoes, washed and halved
1 cup water or chicken/vegetable broth
2 tablespoons butter
2 cloves garlic, minced
1 teaspoon dried rosemary (or your preferred herbs)
Salt and black pepper to taste
Chopped fresh parsley for garnish

Instructions:

Prep the Potatoes:
Wash the baby potatoes and cut them in half. No need to peel them.
Sauté Garlic and Butter
Turn on the Instant Pot's "Sauté" function and melt the butter.
Add the minced garlic and sauté for about 1 minute until fragrant.
Add Potatoes and Seasonings:
Add the halved baby potatoes to the Instant Pot.
Sprinkle with dried rosemary, salt, and black pepper.
Add Liquid:
Pour in the water or broth. The liquid should cover the bottom of the Instant Pot.
Pressure Cook:
Close the Instant Pot lid and set the valve to the "Sealing" position.
Select the "Manual" or "Pressure Cook" function and set the timer for 4-5 minutes (depending on the size of your potatoes). Use the "High Pressure" setting.
Quick Release and Open Lid:
Once the cooking time is up, perform a quick pressure release by carefully turning the valve to "Venting."
When the pressure has released and the float valve drops, carefully open the lid.
Sauté (Optional):
If you prefer a bit of crispiness, you can use the "Sauté" function for a few minutes, stirring occasionally, until the potatoes are slightly golden and crispy.
Serve and Garnish:
Transfer the cooked potatoes to a serving dish.
Garnish with chopped fresh parsley.
Serve and Enjoy:
Instant Pot baby potatoes are ready to be served as a delicious side dish alongside your main course.
These Instant Pot baby potatoes are tender, flavorful, and infused with the aromatic butter and garlic.
They make a perfect accompaniment to various meals, from grilled meats to roasted chicken.

# Crispy Broad Bean Skins

Ingredients:

Fresh broad bean pods (fava beans)
Olive oil
Salt and seasonings of your choice (such as chili powder, paprika, garlic powder, etc.)

Instructions:

Prepare the Broad Bean Pods:
Choose fresh broad bean pods that are plump and bright green in color.
Wash the pods thoroughly and pat them dry with a clean kitchen towel.
Remove the Beans from the Pods:
Open the pods by gently splitting them along the seam using your fingers or a small knife.
Remove the beans from the pods.
Separate the Skins:
Carefully remove the outer skins (husks) from the beans. You can do this by gently pinching the skin near the end where the bean was attached and sliding it off.
Dry the Skins:
Lay the broad bean skins on a paper towel to remove excess moisture.
Season the Skins:
In a bowl, drizzle the broad bean skins with a bit of olive oil and toss to coat them evenly. This will help the skins become crispy during cooking.
Season the skins with salt and any other seasonings of your choice. You can use chili powder, paprika, garlic powder, or other preferred spices.
Bake or Air Fry:
Preheat your oven to about 350°F (175°C) or your air fryer to a similar temperature.
Spread the seasoned broad bean skins on a baking sheet or in the air fryer basket in a single layer.
Cook to Crispy Perfection:
If using the oven, bake the skins for about 15-20 minutes, flipping them halfway through, until they are crispy and golden.
If using the air fryer, air-fry the skins for about 10-15 minutes, shaking the basket occasionally for even cooking.
Cool and Enjoy:
Once the broad bean skins are crispy, remove them from the oven or air fryer and let them cool for a few minutes.
Serve and Snack:
Serve the crispy broad bean skins as a crunchy snack. They are best enjoyed soon after cooking for maximum crispiness.
Crispy broad bean skins can be a unique and tasty way to enjoy fava beans. They're a great alternative to traditional potato chips and offer a satisfying crunch. Feel free to experiment with different seasonings to create your desired flavor profile.

# Crispy Kale

Ingredients:

1 bunch of kale (about 6-8 large leaves)
1 tablespoon olive oil
Salt and seasoning of your choice (such as garlic powder, nutritional yeast, chili powder, etc.)

Instructions:

Preheat the Oven:
Preheat your oven to 350°F (175°C).
Prepare the Kale Leaves:
Wash the kale leaves thoroughly and pat them dry with a clean kitchen towel or paper towels. Remove the tough stems from the kale leaves. Tear the leaves into bite-sized pieces.
Massage with Olive Oil:
Place the torn kale leaves in a large bowl.
Drizzle the olive oil over the kale leaves.
Gently massage the leaves with your hands to ensure they are evenly coated with oil. This helps to make them crispy.
Season the Kale:
Sprinkle salt and your choice of seasoning over the kale leaves. You can use garlic powder, nutritional yeast, chili powder, or any other preferred seasonings.
Arrange on Baking Sheet:
Line a baking sheet with parchment paper.
Arrange the seasoned kale leaves in a single layer on the baking sheet. Avoid overcrowding to ensure crispiness.
Bake in the Oven:
Place the baking sheet in the preheated oven and bake for about 10-15 minutes, or until the kale leaves are crisp and slightly golden. Keep an eye on them as they can burn quickly.
Cool and Enjoy:
Once the kale chips are crispy, remove them from the oven and let them cool on the baking sheet for a few minutes.
Serve and Snack:
Transfer the crispy kale chips to a serving bowl.
Enjoy them as a healthy and flavorful snack!

# Roast Brussels sprouts

Ingredients:

1/2 pound Brussels sprouts, trimmed and halved
2 tablespoons olive oil
Salt and black pepper to taste

Instructions:
Preheat the Oven:
Preheat your oven to 400°F (200°C).
Prep the Brussels Sprouts:
Trim the ends of the Brussels sprouts and cut them in half.
Toss with Oil and Seasoning:
In a bowl, toss the halved Brussels sprouts with olive oil, salt, and black pepper until they are well coated.
Roast in the Oven:
Spread the Brussels sprouts on a baking sheet in a single layer.
Roast:
Roast the Brussels sprouts in the preheated oven for about 20-25 minutes, stirring halfway through, until they are crispy on the edges and tender on the inside.
Serve:
Transfer the roasted Brussels sprouts to a serving dish and enjoy as a delightful side!

# Chargrilled courgettes with lemon & mint

Ingredients:

2 medium courgettes (zucchini), sliced lengthwise
2 tablespoons olive oil
Zest of 1 lemon
Juice of 1 lemon
2 tablespoons fresh mint leaves, chopped
Salt and black pepper to taste

Instructions:
Preheat the Grill or Grill Pan:
Preheat an outdoor grill or stovetop grill pan over medium-high heat.
Prepare the Courgettes:
Slice the courgettes lengthwise into thin strips. You can also slice them diagonally for a different presentation.
Season the Courgettes:
In a bowl, combine the olive oil, lemon zest, lemon juice, chopped mint, salt, and black pepper.
Coat with Marinade:
Place the sliced courgettes in the bowl with the marinade. Toss them gently to coat them evenly with the mixture.
Grill the Courgettes:
Place the marinated courgette slices on the preheated grill or grill pan. Grill for about 2-3 minutes on each side, or until they have distinct grill marks and are tender but not overly soft.
Serve:
Transfer the chargrilled courgettes to a serving platter.
Garnish:
Sprinkle some additional chopped mint over the top for extra freshness and flavor.
Serve and Enjoy:
Serve the chargrilled courgettes with lemon and mint as a delightful side dish. They pair well with grilled meats, fish, or as part of a Mediterranean-inspired meal.

# Vegetable kebabs

Ingredients:

For the Marinade:
2 tablespoons olive oil
2 tablespoons balsamic vinegar
1 teaspoon honey or maple syrup
1 teaspoon Dijon mustard
1 clove garlic, minced
1 teaspoon dried herbs (such as thyme, oregano, or rosemary)
Salt and black pepper to taste

For the Kebabs:

Assorted vegetables, such as bell peppers, red onion, zucchini, cherry tomatoes, and mushrooms, cut into bite-sized pieces
Wooden or metal skewers

Instructions:

Prepare the Marinade:
In a bowl, whisk together the olive oil, balsamic vinegar, honey or maple syrup, Dijon mustard, minced garlic, dried herbs, salt, and black pepper. This will be your marinade.

Prepare the Vegetables:
Cut the assorted vegetables into bite-sized pieces. Keep in mind that the vegetables should be similar in size to ensure even cooking.

Marinate the Vegetables:
Place the cut vegetables in a shallow dish or a resealable plastic bag.
Pour the marinade over the vegetables and toss gently to coat them well. Allow them to marinate for about 15-30 minutes.

Preheat the Grill:
Preheat an outdoor grill or stovetop grill pan over medium-high heat.

Assemble the Kebabs:
Thread the marinated vegetables onto the skewers, alternating the different types of vegetables for a colorful presentation.

Grill the Kebabs:
Place the vegetable kebabs on the preheated grill. Cook for about 10-15 minutes, turning the kebabs occasionally, until the vegetables are tender and have nice grill marks.

Serve:
Carefully remove the kebabs from the grill and transfer them to a serving platter.

Garnish and Enjoy:
Garnish the vegetable kebabs with some fresh herbs, if desired.
Serve the kebabs as a tasty and vibrant dish. They can be served on their own, with rice, or alongside your favorite dipping sauce.

# Chocolate mousse with salted caramel

Ingredients:

For the Chocolate Mousse:
2/3 cup heavy cream
3 ounces semi-sweet or dark chocolate, chopped
1 tablespoon unsalted butter
1/2 teaspoon vanilla extract
Pinch of salt

For the Salted Caramel:
1/4 cup granulated sugar
2 tablespoons unsalted butter
2 tablespoons heavy cream
1/4 teaspoon sea salt (adjust to taste)

Instructions:

Prepare the Chocolate Mousse:

In a heatproof bowl, melt the chopped chocolate and butter together. You can do this over a pot of simmering water or in the microwave in short bursts, stirring until smooth.
Stir in the vanilla extract and a pinch of salt into the melted chocolate mixture. Allow it to cool slightly.
Whip the Cream:
In a separate bowl, whip the heavy cream until soft peaks form.
Gently fold the whipped cream into the melted chocolate mixture until well combined. Be gentle to maintain the mousse's light texture.
Divide the chocolate mousse mixture into two serving glasses or bowls.
Refrigerate the mousse for at least 1-2 hours, or until it's set and chilled.
Prepare the Salted Caramel:
In a small saucepan, melt the granulated sugar over medium heat. Stir constantly until the sugar melts and turns amber in color.
Add the butter to the melted sugar and stir until the butter is fully melted and combined.
Remove the saucepan from heat and carefully add the heavy cream while stirring. The mixture will bubble up.
:
Stir in the sea salt until well incorporated. Taste and adjust the saltiness to your preference.
Allow the salted caramel sauce to cool slightly before using.
When the chocolate mousse is set, drizzle the prepared salted caramel sauce over the top of each mousse.
Serve the chocolate mousse with salted caramel immediately for a delightful combination of rich chocolate and sweet-salty caramel flavors.

# Easy lemon meringue pie

Ingredients:

For the Pie Filling:
1 ready-made 9-inch pie crust (pre-baked and cooled)
1/2 cup granulated sugar
3 tablespoons cornstarch
1/8 teaspoon salt
1 cup water
3 large egg yolks
Zest of 1 lemon
1/4 cup freshly squeezed lemon juice
2 tablespoons unsalted butter

For the Meringue:

3 large egg whites
1/4 teaspoon cream of tartar
6 tablespoons granulated sugar

Instructions:

Prepare the Filling:
In a saucepan, whisk together the sugar, cornstarch, and salt.
Gradually whisk in the water until smooth.
Cook over medium heat, stirring constantly, until the mixture thickens and comes to a boil.
In a separate bowl, whisk the egg yolks. Gradually add a small amount of the hot sugar mixture to the yolks while whisking continuously to temper them.
Pour the tempered egg yolk mixture back into the saucepan and cook over medium heat, stirring constantly, until the mixture thickens further.
Remove from heat and stir in the lemon zest, lemon juice, and butter until the butter is melted and the mixture is smooth.
Assemble the Pie:
Pour the lemon filling into the pre-baked pie crust.
In a clean, dry mixing bowl, beat the egg whites and cream of tartar until soft peaks form.
Gradually add the sugar while continuing to beat until stiff peaks form.
Spread the meringue over the lemon filling, making sure to spread it all the way to the edges of the crust to seal in the filling.
Preheat the oven to 350°F (175°C).
Place the pie in the oven and bake for about 10-15 minutes, or until the meringue is golden brown.
Allow the pie to cool completely before slicing and serving.

# Baked ricotta cake

Ingredients:

1 cup ricotta cheese
1/4 cup granulated sugar
1 large egg
1 teaspoon vanilla extract
Zest of 1 lemon
1/4 cup all-purpose flour
1/4 teaspoon baking powder
Pinch of salt
Powdered sugar, for dusting
Fresh berries, for garnish
(optional)

Instructions:

Preheat the Oven:
Preheat your oven to 350°F (175°C).
Grease and lightly flour a small round baking dish (about 6 inches in diameter) or individual ramekins.
Prepare the Ricotta Mixture:
In a mixing bowl, whisk together the ricotta cheese, granulated sugar, egg, vanilla extract, and lemon zest until smooth and well combined.
Add Dry Ingredients:
Gradually sift in the all-purpose flour, baking powder, and a pinch of salt. Gently fold the dry ingredients into the ricotta mixture until just combined. Be careful not to overmix.
Bake the Cake:
Pour the batter into the prepared baking dish or ramekins.
Bake:
Place the baking dish or ramekins in the preheated oven and bake for about 25-30 minutes, or until the cake is set and lightly golden on top.
Cool:
Once baked, remove the cake from the oven and let it cool in the baking dish or ramekins for a few minutes.
Serve:
If using a single baking dish, you can serve the cake directly from it. If using ramekins, gently run a knife around the edges to loosen the cake before transferring it to a serving plate.
Dust with Powdered Sugar:
Dust the top of the baked ricotta cake with powdered sugar for a touch of sweetness and decoration.
Garnish and Enjoy:
Garnish the cake with fresh berries, if desired, for a burst of color and flavor.
This baked ricotta cake offers a creamy texture with a subtle hint of lemon and vanilla. It's a simple and elegant dessert option for two, perfect for sharing after a delicious meal.

# Almond and honey cake

Ingredients:

1/2 cup almond flour
1/4 cup all-purpose flour
1/2 teaspoon baking powder
1/8 teaspoon salt
1/4 cup unsalted butter, softened
1/4 cup granulated sugar
1 large egg
2 tablespoons honey
1/2 teaspoon vanilla extract
Sliced almonds, for topping
Powdered sugar, for dusting

Instructions:

Preheat the Oven:
Preheat your oven to 350°F (175°C).
Grease and lightly flour a small round cake pan (about 6 inches in diameter) or individual ramekins.
Mix Dry ngredients:

In a bowl, whisk together the almond flour, all-purpose flour, baking powder, and salt. Set aside.
Cream Butter and Sugar:
In a separate mixing bowl, cream together the softened butter and granulated sugar until light and fluffy.
Add Wet Ingredients:
Beat in the egg until well incorporated.
Add the honey and vanilla extract and mix until smooth.
Combine Dry and Wet Ingredients:
Gradually add the dry ingredient mixture to the wet ingredients, stirring until just combined.
Be careful not to overmix.
Pour the cake batter into the prepared cake pan or divide it evenly among individual ramekins.
Sprinkle a layer of sliced almonds over the top of the cake batter. Press them lightly into the batter.
Place the cake pan or ramekins in the preheated oven and bake for about 20-25 minutes, or until the cake is golden brown and a toothpick inserted into the center comes out clean.
Cool and Dust with Powdered Sugar:
Once baked, remove the cake from the oven and let it cool in the pan or ramekins for a few minutes.
Carefully transfer the cake to a serving plate and let it cool completely.
Dust the top of the cake with powdered sugar for a sweet finishing touch.
Slice the almond and honey cake and serve it as a delightful dessert for two. It pairs wonderfully with a cup of tea or coffee.

# Frozen caramel slice

Ingredients:

For the Crust:
1/2 cup graham cracker crumbs (or biscuit crumbs)
2 tablespoons unsalted butter, melted

For the Chocolate Layer:

1/2 cup chocolate chips (semi-sweet or milk chocolate)
1 tablespoon unsalted butter

For the Caramel Layer:

1/2 cup sweetened condensed milk
1/4 cup caramel sauce (store-bought or homemade)
Pinch of salt

Instructions:

Prepare the Crust:
Crush the Crumbs:
In a bowl, crush graham crackers or biscuits into fine crumbs. You can use a food processor or place them in a zip-top bag and crush them with a rolling pin.
Mix the melted butter with the graham cracker crumbs until the crumbs are evenly coated.
Assemble the Base:
Divide the crumb mixture between two small individual dessert dishes or ramekins.
Press the crumbs down firmly to create an even crust layer.
Mix Caramel Ingredients:
In a bowl, combine the sweetened condensed milk, caramel sauce, and a pinch of salt. Mix until well combined.
Divide the caramel mixture equally between the two dessert dishes, spreading it over the crust.
Prepare the Chocolate Layer:
In a microwave-safe bowl or using a double boiler, melt the chocolate chips and unsalted butter together until smooth.
Pour the melted chocolate mixture over the caramel layer in each dish, spreading it evenly.
Chill in the Freezer:
Place the dessert dishes in the freezer and let them freeze for at least 2-3 hours, or until they are firm.
Once the frozen caramel slices are firm, remove them from the freezer.
Let them sit at room temperature for a few minutes to soften slightly before enjoying.

# Strawberry and rhubarb cobbler

Ingredients:

For the Fruit Filling:
1 cup strawberries, hulled and sliced
1 cup rhubarb, chopped into 1/2-inch pieces
1/4 cup granulated sugar
2 tablespoons cornstarch
1/2 teaspoon vanilla extract
Zest of 1 lemon

For the Cobbler Topping:
1/2 cup all-purpose flour
2 tablespoons granulated sugar
1/2 teaspoon baking powder
1/8 teaspoon salt
2 tablespoons unsalted butter, cold and cubed
3 tablespoons milk (dairy or non-dairy)

Instructions:
Preheat the Oven:
Preheat your oven to 375°F (190°C).
In a bowl, combine the sliced strawberries, chopped rhubarb, granulated sugar, cornstarch, vanilla extract, and lemon zest. Gently toss to coat the fruit evenly with the mixture.
Divide the fruit mixture between two small baking dishes or ramekins.
In a separate bowl, whisk together the flour, granulated sugar, baking powder, and salt.
Using a pastry cutter or your fingers, cut in the cold, cubed butter into the dry mixture until the mixture resembles coarse crumbs.
Add the milk and stir until just combined. The dough will be sticky.
Divide the cobbler dough into two portions. Drop spoonfuls of the dough over the fruit filling in the baking dishes.
Place the baking dishes on a baking sheet to catch any potential drips.
Bake in the preheated oven for about 25-30 minutes, or until the fruit filling is bubbling and the cobbler topping is golden brown.
Remove the cobbler from the oven and let it cool slightly before serving.
Serve the strawberry and rhubarb cobbler warm, either on its own or with a scoop of vanilla ice cream or a dollop of whipped cream.

# Cherry and almond crumble

Ingredients:

For the Filling:
2 cups fresh or frozen cherries, pitted
2 tablespoons granulated sugar
1 tablespoon cornstarch
1 tablespoon lemon juice

For the Crumble Topping:
1/3 cup all-purpose flour
1/4 cup old-fashioned rolled oats
1/4 cup sliced almonds
2 tablespoons brown sugar
1/4 teaspoon ground cinnamon
Pinch of salt
3 tablespoons unsalted butter,
cold and cut into small cubes

Instructions:

Preheat the Oven:
Preheat your oven to 375°F (190°C).
Prepare the Filling:
In a bowl, combine the pitted cherries, granulated sugar, cornstarch, and lemon juice. Toss gently to coat the cherries evenly. If using frozen cherries, let them thaw slightly before using.
Assemble the Crumble Topping:
In a separate bowl, mix together the all-purpose flour, rolled oats, sliced almonds, brown sugar, ground cinnamon, and a pinch of salt.
Add the cold butter cubes to the mixture and use your fingers or a fork to work the butter into the dry ingredients. Mix until the mixture resembles coarse crumbs.
Assemble the Crumble:
Divide the cherry filling evenly between two individual ramekins or oven-safe dishes.
Add the Topping:
Sprinkle the crumble topping over the cherry filling, covering it completely.
Bake the Crumbles:
Place the ramekins on a baking sheet to catch any drips. Bake in the preheated oven for about 25-30 minutes, or until the topping is golden brown and the filling is bubbling.
Cool and Serve:
Allow the cherry and almond crumbles to cool slightly before serving. The filling will thicken as it cools.
Enjoy:
Serve the cherry and almond crumbles warm, either on their own or with a scoop of vanilla ice cream or a dollop of whipped cream.

# Apple, berry and port crumble

Ingredients:

For the Filling:
2 apples, peeled, cored, and sliced
1 cup mixed berries (such as strawberries, blueberries, raspberries)
2 tablespoons granulated sugar
1 tablespoon cornstarch
2 tablespoons port wine (or apple juice)

For the Crumble Topping:

1/3 cup all-purpose flour
1/4 cup old-fashioned rolled oats
1/4 cup chopped walnuts or pecans
2 tablespoons brown sugar
1/4 teaspoon ground cinnamon
Pinch of salt
3 tablespoons unsalted butter, cold and cut into small cubes

Instructions:

Preheat the Oven:

Preheat your oven to 375°F (190°C).
Prepare the Filling:
In a bowl, combine the sliced apples, mixed berries, granulated sugar, cornstarch, and port wine. Gently toss to coat the fruit evenly.
Assemble the Crumble Topping:
In a separate bowl, mix together the all-purpose flour, rolled oats, chopped walnuts or pecans, brown sugar, ground cinnamon, and a pinch of salt.
Add the cold butter cubes to the mixture and use your fingers or a fork to work the butter into the dry ingredients. Mix until the mixture resembles coarse crumbs.
Assemble the Crumble:
Divide the apple and berry filling evenly between two individual ramekins or oven-safe dishes.
Add the Topping:
Sprinkle the crumble topping over the fruit filling, covering it completely.
Bake the Crumbles:
Place the ramekins on a baking sheet to catch any drips. Bake in the preheated oven for about 25-30 minutes, or until the topping is golden brown and the filling is bubbling.
Allow the apple, berry, and port crumbles to cool slightly before serving.
Serve the crumbles warm, either on their own or with a scoop of vanilla ice cream or a dollop of whipped cream.

# Crumble cake with berries

For the Cake:

1/2 cup all-purpose flour
1/4 cup granulated sugar
1/2 teaspoon baking powder
Pinch of salt
1/4 cup unsalted butter, softened
1 large egg
1/4 teaspoon vanilla extract
2 tablespoons milk

For the Berry Filling:
1 cup mixed berries (such as blueberries, raspberries, strawberries)
1 tablespoon granulated sugar
1 teaspoon lemon juice

For the Crumble Topping:

1/4 cup all-purpose flour
2 tablespoons granulated sugar
2 tablespoons unsalted butter, cold and cut into small cubes

Instructions:

Preheat the Oven:
Preheat your oven to 350°F (175°C). Grease a small baking dish or two individual ramekins.
In a bowl, mix the mixed berries with granulated sugar and lemon juice. Toss gently to coat the berries, then set aside.
In a bowl, combine the all-purpose flour and granulated sugar for the crumble topping.
Add the cold butter cubes and use your fingers to work the butter into the dry ingredients until crumbly. Set aside.
In a separate bowl, whisk together the all-purpose flour, granulated sugar, baking powder, and a pinch of salt.
Add the softened butter, egg, vanilla extract, and milk. Mix until well combined and smooth.
Pour the cake batter into the greased baking dish or ramekins, spreading it evenly.
Add the Berry Filling:
Spoon the mixed berry filling over the cake batter, distributing the berries evenly.
Add the Crumble Topping:
Sprinkle the crumble topping over the berry filling, covering it evenly.
Bake the Crumble Cake:
Bake in the preheated oven for about 25-30 minutes, or until the cake is golden brown and a toothpick inserted into the cake portion comes out clean.
Allow the crumble cake to cool slightly before serving.
Serve the crumble cake warm, either on its own or with a dollop of whipped cream or a scoop of vanilla ice cream.

# Gingerbread brownies

Ingredients:

For the Brownie Batter:
1/4 cup unsalted butter
1/3 cup granulated sugar
1/4 cup molasses
1 large egg
1/2 teaspoon vanilla extract
1/2 cup all-purpose flour
1/2 teaspoon ground ginger
1/2 teaspoon ground cinnamon
1/4 teaspoon ground nutmeg
1/4 teaspoon baking powder
Pinch of salt

For the Gingerbread Frosting:
2 tablespoons cream cheese, softened
2 tablespoons unsalted butter, softened
1/2 cup powdered sugar
1/2 teaspoon ground ginger
1/2 teaspoon vanilla extract

Instructions:

Preheat the Oven:
Preheat your oven to 350°F (175°C). Grease a small baking dish or individual ramekins.
Prepare the Brownie Batter:
In a microwave-safe bowl, melt the butter. Stir in the granulated sugar and molasses until well combined.
Let the mixture cool slightly, then whisk in the egg and vanilla extract.
Mix Dry Ingredients:
In a separate bowl, whisk together the all-purpose flour, ground ginger, ground cinnamon, ground nutmeg, baking powder, and a pinch of salt.
Combine Wet and Dry Ingredients:
Gradually add the dry ingredient mixture to the wet ingredients, stirring until just combined.
Pour the brownie batter into the greased baking dish or ramekins, spreading it evenly.
Bake in the preheated oven for about 20-25 minutes, or until a toothpick inserted into the center comes out with a few moist crumbs.
Prepare the Gingerbread Frosting:
In a bowl, beat together the softened cream cheese and softened butter until smooth.
Add the powdered sugar, ground ginger, and vanilla extract. Mix until creamy and well combined.
Once the brownies have cooled, spread the gingerbread frosting over the top
Cut the brownies into squares and serve the Gingerbread Brownies as a delightful dessert for two.

# Nutella cheesecake

Ingredients:

For the Crust:
1/2 cup graham cracker crumbs
2 tablespoons unsalted butter, melted
1 tablespoon granulated sugar

For the Cheesecake Filling:
8 oz (225g) cream cheese, softened
1/4 cup Nutella
1/4 cup granulated sugar
1 large egg
1/2 teaspoon vanilla extract

For the Topping (Optional):

Whipped cream
Chopped hazelnuts or chocolate shavings

Instructions:

Preheat the Oven:
Preheat your oven to 325°F (165°C).
Prepare the Crust:
In a bowl, combine the graham cracker crumbs, melted butter, and granulated sugar. Mix until the crumbs are evenly coated with butter.
Assemble the Crust
Press the crumb mixture into the bottom of two individual ramekins, creating an even crust layer.
Prepare the Cheesecake Filling:
In a mixing bowl, beat the softened cream cheese until smooth.
Add Nutella and Sugar
Add the Nutella and granulated sugar to the cream cheese. Beat until well combined and creamy.
Beat in the egg and vanilla extract until the mixture is smooth and well incorporated.
Fill the Ramekins:
Divide the cheesecake filling evenly between the two prepared crusts in the ramekins.
Place the ramekins on a baking sheet and bake in the preheated oven for about 20-25 minutes, or until the cheesecake is set but still slightly jiggly in the center.
Remove the ramekins from the oven and let the cheesecakes cool to room temperature. Then, cover them and refrigerate for a few hours or until fully chilled and set.
Just before serving, you can top each cheesecake with a dollop of whipped cream and a sprinkle of chopped hazelnuts or chocolate shavings.
Indulge in the rich and creamy Nutella Cheesecakes as a delightful treat for two.
These Nutella Cheesecakes are a decadent and satisfying dessert that's perfect for sharing. The Nutella adds a luscious hazelnut-chocolate flavor to the creamy cheesecake, making every bite a delight.

# Spiced pumpkin pie

Ingredients:

For the Pie Crust:
1 store-bought or homemade pie crust
(enough for a single crust)
For the Pumpkin Filling:

1/2 cup canned pumpkin puree
1/4 cup granulated sugar
1/4 teaspoon ground cinnamon
1/8 teaspoon ground nutmeg
1/8 teaspoon ground ginger
1/8 teaspoon ground cloves
Pinch of salt
1/4 cup evaporated milk
1 large egg

Instructions:

Preheat the Oven:
Preheat your oven to 350°F (175°C).
Prepare the Pie Crust:
If using a store-bought pie crust, follow the package instructions for pre-baking the crust. If using a homemade crust, roll it out and fit it into a small pie dish or two individual ramekins.
In a bowl, whisk together the canned pumpkin puree, granulated sugar, ground cinnamon, ground nutmeg, ground ginger, ground cloves, and a pinch of salt.
Add Evaporated Milk and Egg:
Gradually whisk in the evaporated milk until the mixture is smooth.
Beat in the egg until well combined.
Pour into the Crust:
Pour the spiced pumpkin filling into the pre-baked pie crust or divided evenly between the individual ramekins.
Bake the Pie:
Place the pie dish or ramekins on a baking sheet to catch any spills. Bake in the preheated oven for about 20-25 minutes, or until the filling is set around the edges and slightly jiggly in the center.
Cool and Serve:
Remove the pie or ramekins from the oven and let them cool to room temperature. Then, cover and refrigerate for a few hours or until fully chilled and set.
Serve the Spiced Pumpkin Pie slices on plates or enjoy the individual pumpkin pies directly from the ramekins.
Top each slice or serving with a dollop of whipped cream for an extra touch of indulgence.
Savor the warm and comforting flavors of the Spiced Pumpkin Pie as a delightful dessert for two.

# Spiced cherry and strawberry pie

Ingredients:
For the Pie Crust:
1 store-bought or homemade pie crust
(enough for a single crust)
For the Filling:
1 cup pitted and halved cherries
1 cup sliced strawberries
1/4 cup granulated sugar
1 tablespoon cornstarch
1/2 teaspoon ground cinnamon
1/4 teaspoon ground nutmeg
Pinch of salt
1/2 teaspoon vanilla extract

For the Topping:

1/4 cup all-purpose flour
2 tablespoons granulated sugar
2 tablespoons unsalted butter, cold and cut into small cubes

Instructions:

Preheat the Oven:
Preheat your oven to 375°F (190°C).
Prepare the Pie Crust:
If using a store-bought pie crust, follow the package instructions for pre-baking the crust. If using a homemade crust, roll it out and fit it into a small pie dish.
Prepare the Filling:
In a bowl, combine the halved cherries, sliced strawberries, granulated sugar, cornstarch, ground cinnamon, ground nutmeg, pinch of salt, and vanilla extract. Toss gently to coat the fruit with the spices and sugar.
Assemble the Pie:
Transfer the spiced cherry and strawberry filling into the prepared pie crust.
Prepare the Topping
In a separate bowl, mix together the all-purpose flour and granulated sugar for the topping. Add the cold butter cubes and use your fingers to work the butter into the dry ingredients until crumbly.
Add the Topping:
Sprinkle the crumble topping over the fruit filling, covering it evenly.
Bake the Pie:
Place the pie dish on a baking sheet to catch any drips. Bake in the preheated oven for about 25-30 minutes, or until the filling is bubbling and the topping is golden brown.
Allow the pie to cool slightly before serving.
Serve slices of the Spiced Cherry and Strawberry Pie on plates.
Optional Topping:
Top each slice with a scoop of vanilla ice cream or a dollop of whipped cream for an extra touch of indulgence.

# Lemon and finger lime tart

Ingredients:

For the Tart Crust:
1 store-bought or homemade tart crust (enough for a small tart pan)
For the Lemon and Finger Lime Filling:
2 large eggs
1/2 cup granulated sugar
Zest of 1 lemon
1/4 cup freshly squeezed lemon juice
1 tablespoon finger lime pearls (substitute regular lime zest if unavailable)
2 tablespoons unsalted butter, melted and cooled
For Garnish:
Whipped cream or whipped coconut cream
Additional finger lime pearls or lemon zest

Instructions:

Preheat the Oven:
Preheat your oven according to the temperature specified on the tart crust package or recipe.
Prepare the Tart Crust:
If using a store-bought tart crust, follow the package instructions for pre-baking. If using a homemade crust, roll it out and fit it into a small tart pan. Pre-bake the crust according to your recipe or until it's lightly golden.
Prepare the Lemon and Finger Lime Filling:
In a bowl, whisk together the eggs and granulated sugar until well combined.
Add Lemon and Finger Lime Flavor:
Add the lemon zest, freshly squeezed lemon juice, and finger lime pearls (or lime zest). Mix until incorporated.
Incorporate Melted Butter:
Gradually pour in the melted and cooled butter while continuously whisking the mixture. Pour the lemon and finger lime filling into the pre-baked tart crust.
Bake the Tart:
Place the tart pan on a baking sheet to catch any spills. Bake in the preheated oven for about 15-20 minutes, or until the filling is set and slightly jiggly in the center.
Cool and Chill:
Remove the tart from the oven and let it cool to room temperature. Once cooled, cover the tart and refrigerate for a few hours to fully chill and set.
Garnish and Serve:
Before serving, garnish the Lemon and Finger Lime Tart with whipped cream or whipped coconut cream, and additional finger lime pearls or lemon zest.
Enjoy:
Slice and savor the delightful flavors of the Lemon and Finger Lime Tart as a refreshing and tangy dessert for two.

# Apple, Pecan, and Maple Syrup Crumble

Ingredients:

For the Apple Filling:
2 medium apples, peeled, cored, and sliced
2 tablespoons granulated sugar
1 tablespoon lemon juice
1/2 teaspoon ground cinnamon
Pinch of ground nutmeg
Pinch of salt

For the Crumble Topping:

1/4 cup all-purpose flour
1/4 cup old-fashioned rolled oats
2 tablespoons chopped pecans
2 tablespoons brown sugar
1/4 teaspoon ground cinnamon
Pinch of salt
2 tablespoons unsalted butter, cold and cut into small cubes

Instructions:

Preheat the Oven:
Preheat your oven to 375°F (190°C).
Prepare the Apple Filling:
In a bowl, combine the sliced apples, granulated sugar, lemon juice, ground cinnamon, ground nutmeg, and a pinch of salt. Toss gently to coat the apples evenly with the spices and sugar.
Assemble the Crumble Topping:
In a separate bowl, mix together the all-purpose flour, rolled oats, chopped pecans, brown sugar, ground cinnamon, and a pinch of salt.
Add the cold butter cubes and use your fingers to work the butter into the dry ingredients until crumbly.
Divide the apple filling evenly between two individual ramekins or oven-safe dishes.
Sprinkle the crumble topping over the apple filling, covering it evenly.
Bake the Crumbles:
Place the ramekins on a baking sheet to catch any drips. Bake in the preheated oven for about 20-25 minutes, or until the topping is golden brown and the apple filling is bubbling.
Allow the apple, pecan, and maple syrup crumbles to cool slightly before serving.
Serve the crumbles warm, either on their own or with a scoop of vanilla ice cream or a dollop of whipped cream.
Enjoy the comforting flavors of the Apple, Pecan, and Maple Syrup Crumble as a delightful dessert for two.

Thank you for choosing to embark on this culinary journey with me and for entrusting me with a small part of your kitchen adventures.

Your support and trust mean the world to me. Every recipe, every technique, and every story shared in this cookbook is a reflection of my passion for food and my desire to bring joy to your tables. Your decision to purchase this cookbook not only encourages me to continue sharing my culinary knowledge but also supports the countless hours of recipe testing, writing, and photography that went into its creation.

## Wishing you many happy moments of deliciousness and culinary creativity!

### For Zian And Milan, who brings smiles to my face and joy to my heart every day

www.ingramcontent.com/pod-product-compliance
Lightning Source LLC
Chambersburg PA
CBHW071319080526
**44587CB00018B/3287**